Thomas G Selby

The Chinaman in His Own Stories

Thomas G Selby

The Chinaman in His Own Stories

ISBN/EAN: 9783337005719

Printed in Europe, USA, Canada, Australia, Japan

Cover: Foto ©Thomas Meinert / pixelio.de

More available books at **www.hansebooks.com**

THE CHINAMAN

IN HIS OWN STORIES

BY

THOMAS G. SELBY

London
CHARLES H. KELLY
2, CASTLE ST., CITY RD., E.C.; AND 66, PATERNOSTER ROW, E.C.
1895

CONTENTS

CHAP.		PAGE
I.	INTRODUCTION	7
II.	KINSHIP AND KINDNESS	17
III.	THE GOOD GRADUATE	48
IV.	THE HAUNTED MELON GARDEN	80
V.	THE DASHING WIFE	87
VI.	MADAM CROSS-GRAIN	106
VII.	THE NINE DEMON INCARNATIONS	171
VIII.	A BUDDHIST'S VISION OF PURGATORY	181

THE CHINAMAN
IN HIS OWN STORIES

CHAPTER I

INTRODUCTION

THESE translations are presented to the English reader with the idea of giving a brief glance at Chinese life through Chinese fiction. In plot the stories are primitive and puerile, and the translator has sometimes doubted whether it was worth while to print them. Chinese names always ruin a Chinese story for the average reader, and yet to give English equivalents is to destroy the piquancy of the narrative, and load it with an insufferable burden of grandiose Johnsonese. In some cases, where it has been possible, the English equivalents of the names have been given, and in other cases the Chinese forms of the names are retained. Over against the simplicity and feebleness of the ruling plots and motives of the tales must be set the fact that they contain a very perceptible salt of humour, and the descriptive power is not infrequently keen and graphic. If the reader should fail to realise this, the fault must be put down to the clumsiness of the translator. The stories may at least amuse children, and if any one will take the trouble to look beyond the elementary art, he will gain some little insight into the thought and life of the wonderful populations of Eastern Asia. Perhaps one of the quickest and most accurate methods of picking up a knowledge of the manners, family and social habits and traditions, philosophies and religions of a foreign nation is to study, as opportunity may offer, its novels and novelettes. Chinese fiction is not rated highly by the Chinese themselves, and hitherto has not attracted to its pursuit minds of genius such as Scott, Eliot, Thackeray, Hawthorne, in the West. Perhaps one explanation of this is the limited repertory of motives with which a Chinese story-teller has to deal, as well as the comparatively narrow range of knowledge and interest in a country where each individual life is lived in a groove occupied by precisely similar lives for thousands of years.

The movement of a Chinese novel does not centre in courtship and marriage, for the simple reason that marriage without courtship is a proceeding in which romance other than that of the lottery is all but impossible. The sexes are rigidly separated, and young men and maidens never meet in drawing-rooms or at picnics, and discover each other's affinities in conversation which starts in metaphysic and ends at the very opposite pole of thought. All marriages are arranged by brokers or go-betweens, who are employed by parents to discover suitable alliances for their children, and who transact the preliminaries of the betrothal. Boys and girls are pledged by their parents to marriage, sometimes within a year or two of their birth, and such covenants are inviolable. The present writer has met with cases in which it has been held illegal to break off the engagement when signs of leprosy or some other loathsome disease had appeared in one of the contracting parties. No misconduct, however flagrant, on the side of the youth at least, is held to be a release from the covenant. The go-betweens consider the status of the families they represent and seek equal status, and the correspondences between the horoscopes of those about to be betrothed are looked upon as conclusive arguments for the union. The children are supposed never to meet or speak to each other, and it would be taste unpardonably bad were the parents representing the one side ever to discuss the subject with those of the other side. These marriage customs despoil the Chinese novelist of his most promising materials. He has to make a picture of family harmony the climax of his tale, and the ingenuities of providential retribution his chief plot. The Chinese Competition Wallah is a wonderful piece of machinery put at the service of the gods; and the man of virtue, heroism, and filial piety always distinguishes himself in the imperial examinations. The reader will not fail to notice the high place given to hall-marked scholarship in these stories. The man who earns a degree may appear to plead his own cause in the courts of the mandarins, and also to represent his fellow clansmen. A clan rejoicing in a large number of graduate names on its roll always feels itself strong, and puts on the airs assumed by the dependents of heroic chieftains in the old Border days.

Some of these Chinaman's tales may possibly be pronounced farcical and extravagant. Men and women are killed and suicides committed upon a scale which out-Haggards some of our own blood-and-thunder novelists. These features are unfortunately only too true to life. In some parts of the country fierce and bloody clan and family feuds go on for years, and the imperial government is too weak, corrupt, or Laodicean to interfere in the internecine strife of the villages. Often enough, a woman gets her own way by threatening to commit suicide; and, often enough, women who have grievances, great or small, and cannot get their own way, do put an end to themselves. There was some truth in the brutal observation made to the present writer by an old American boatswain who had seen many things on a Peruvian coolie ship. "A Chinaman aire that aggrawatin', he'll lie down and die just to wex yer." When a woman who has married into a neighbouring clan dies or commits suicide, her own friends almost always assume she has been neglected in sickness or hounded to suicide, and demand blood-money. Of course there is no true medical science in China, and no registration of deaths upon the basis of medical certificates; and this defect in the Chinese civilisation opens the way to interminable suspicion, heart-burning, and faction. In one of the stories the reader will see the schisms in the home which are almost inseparable from polygamy and concubinage. The Chinaman expects that submission to the established authority of the household will keep the household in peace, but he forgets that he may sometimes be overtaxing the dutifulness of human nature.

Some of these types of virtue are at variance with our ideals of truthfulness and independence. The characters glorified are obsequious to the point of weakness and imbecility. Perhaps we need a little more of the conciliatory spirit which has coined the Chinese proverb, "A soft tongue outlasts the hard teeth"; but the probable verdict upon the Good Graduate, as well as the meek and long-suffering heroine in the story of Madam Cross-grain, will be that they were mere weaklings, for whom little respect can be entertained.

All the stories are of course ruled by the idea that filial piety is the first of virtues, and the duties growing up out of blood brotherhood come next. A Chinese bride must transfer her affections from her own parents, and affect to love and obey her husband's parents in preference to her own. The mother-in-law is the head of the household, and to submit is the first duty not only of her sons, but also of their wives. The wife is married not because her husband wants a compatible companion, but to bear children and to become a servant to the husband's mother. The husband must beat his wife if his parents command him to do so, however well-pleasing to his own affections the wife may happen to be. If he is left a widower, he must marry again if his parents so direct him. During the lifetime of the parents the son has no theoretical right to his own earnings, and should place them at the disposal of his parents. In some cases parents may forego this right, but in the abstract a son is a serf who cannot hold property during their lifetime. If a husband seem to be loving his wife more than his father and mother, that is looked upon as vice of the blackest description. The New Testament precept, "For this cause shall a man leave his father and mother, and shall be joined unto his wife," is one of the chief stumbling-blocks with which the Chinese are confronted in accepting Christianity. A Chinese proverb says: "Parents are like the sun and the moon. If they should be blotted out of the sky, it would be impossible to replace them. A wife is like a garment. When the garment is worn out, it is always possible to buy a new one."

The stories emphasise the doctrine of providential retribution. The conception of justice, as we judge things, is just a little out of focus. The female despot, Madam Cross-grain, gets off very well indeed. Perhaps the Chinese story-teller considers that it was the privilege of her position to make herself as disagreeable as possible, and that rancour in one filling the post of authority is not the vice it would be in one under the yoke. It scarcely accords with our ideas of justice, that the child of a good man adopted by his brother, who was bereaved of his children as the punishment of his offence against the law of filial piety, should share the broken fortunes of his foster-father, and that the children of this adopted child even should have but a meagre inheritance of good fortune to mark their foster-grandfather's delinquencies. The Chinese, however, are accustomed to think of the solidarity of the family and the clan in their succeeding generations rather than of the responsibility of the individual.

The last translation in this series of short stories, "A Buddhist's Vision of Purgatory," will probably be found to possess several features of interest for the English reader. It is not without its value as a testimony to the world-wide belief in a future life and the great retributions that enact themselves there. Chinese students have generally assumed that the elaborate conceptions of purgatory here dramatised for popular study came from India with Buddhism at the beginning of the Christian era, and that Buddhism borrowed the substance of these conceptions from the old Brahmanism of India. Tauism, one of the indigenous religions of China, mysteriously adopted them without acknowledgment at an early but undetermined period, and has since taught them as though they were its own. Not improbably a strongly defined and elaborate belief in retribution after death was part and parcel of the primitive religious tradition of the Chinese race.

The defects of taste present in these delineations must not blind us to that striking belief in an unerring principle of judgment they illustrate. Both here and hereafter vast and mysterious powers reckon with us for our weal or woe. The reader who despises and dismisses these Chinese representations on the ground of their ghastly coarseness will betray superficiality and narrowness, and prove himself quite unfit for the study of the great subject of comparative religion.

In extenuation of the ruthlessness and brutality of these views of punishment, it must be said that local colour necessarily enters into the view of spiritual retribution and the power of conceiving it, and that the vision of the following pages is steeped in the tradition and practice of the Chinese criminal courts.

The genius of the Chinese language has much to do with the gross concrete character of the descriptions given by this Chinese writer. Inflected and alphabetic languages produce a larger stock of terms for the expression of abstract and spiritual ideas than ideographic languages. The ideographic language we may compare to the old line engravings. They are full of sharp definition, and do not lend themselves to vague suggestions and atmospheric effects.

The inflected and alphabetic language we may compare to the method of producing those tender and dainty illustrations which appear from time to time in some of our illustrated magazines. After the picture has been drawn or photographed, it is half sponged out, so that the fine aerial effects which excite our wonder are produced. In the non-ideographic languages it is possible for a word to lose its sharp edge and become a dim suggestion of spiritual things. In such a language as the Chinese, where a word is represented by a character in which there is a pictorial feature still present, the word cannot lose its outline, and must remain a sharp picture to the very end of its history. And it is impossible to eliminate the concreteness from an idea unless you can eliminate the ideographic element from the character which expresses it. The sharp, abrupt, unsoftened line of the Chinese ideograph is adverse to vague mysticism of speech, and compels perhaps the gross, repulsive realism of these descriptions.

In the closing scene of this vision it will be observed that the Chinese writer anticipates the doctrine of the theosophists, and indeed of our mediæval astrologers, about the astral body. Multiplex souls are supposed to inhere in the same personality, and may become temporarily separated from each other and transported into distant realms, whilst the body continues in life and maintains its common functions. For good or for evil the consciousness may bifurcate, and one stream of it may pass into some strange plane aloof from that in which the living form moves and acts. The theory has a close relation to the speculations of that occult psychology which assumes that the centre of consciousness may be transferred to some point outside the body.

CHAPTER II

KINSHIP AND KINDNESS—A CHINESE FARCE
WITH A MORAL

PERSONÆ.

HAK TAK and TSUN TAK, two brothers.
HAK TAK'S WIFE.
CASH and PETTYMAN, two worthless companions.

TWO sons named Hak Tak and Tsun Tak (Capacity and Achievement) comprised the little family of Mr. Ming, of the Heung Shan district of Kwangtung. Through the early death of their father, these two youths came into the possession of a small estate worth four or five thousand dollars. A girl, whose maiden name was Lin, and who proved herself true, strong, and clear-judging, deferential to her lord, and affable to her young brother-in-law, became the bride of Hak Tak. Tsun Tak, who was between seventeen and eighteen years of age, at the time of this story was unmarried, and occupied himself with the work of the ancestral farm.

The elder brother was on terms of effusive intimacy with two men called Ts'in and Ts'iu (Cash and Pettyman), who were fertile in plots, without settled employment, and accustomed to cultivate the forms of friendship for the food and drink that came to them in this way. At the outset, Hak Tak was quite blind to the sordidness of their motives, inasmuch as he was hoodwinked and overborne by outbursts of affected sympathy on the part of Mr. Cash, and the gross flatteries of Mr. Pettyman. Both acquaintances had a dash of piquancy about them, and talked perpetually about "The History of the Three Capitals and the Seven States," describing, with great animation, strokes of genius and wonderful exploits and adventures.

Upon receiving any imaginary slight or offence, Hak Tak, who was somewhat unamiable by temperament used to wax hot with indignation. Cash and Pettyman, instead of slaking down with timely supplies of water the kindling flames, only poured on oil. "You have nothing to fear. Such an affront is intolerable, and you might even venture to pommel him upon your own responsibility. It would be the easiest matter in the world to make your grievance the ground of a successful lawsuit." Cash would then chime in that his sister's husband was a small military mandarin and had influence, and Pettyman would add that he could claim as a distant relative an official of very high rank indeed. Thereupon Hak Tak would clap his hands and say, "These things being so, we may spin the heavens round at will," pouring out with the word a full cup of wine for Cash, and addressing him as "Pink of Allies," and yet another cup for Pettyman, apostrophising him as "Pearl of Brothers." Thus the three would drink merrily together, and stretch their mouths in loud songs, rubbing their fists in menace of distant antagonists, and laughing with boisterous vulgarity.

At such times Hak Tak would call out at the pitch of his voice: "My younger brothers are all come; be quick and make hot some *samshoo*. If you have not time to kill and cook a fowl, beat up twenty ducks' eggs and cook them with half a pound of dried shrimps; and mince a pound of salt pork, and make a quick fire, and wash the small rice-pan. Be sharp with that frizzle."

But Tsun Tak was not entirely pleased at these proceedings and the constant visits of Cash and Pettyman, with the upset occasioned in the house; and the torrents of vapid, unprofitable talk evidently irritated him. Little by little his displeasure began to leak out.

One day, when Cash and Pettyman called, the elder brother was away from home, and the younger did not accord them a sufficiently hearty reception, from their point of view at least. A short time after, as Cash and Pettyman were drinking wine with Hak Tak, Cash said, with a smile: "You carry yourself in the world like the first-rate fellow you are. Kindness is the one idea you keep in view, and in your intercourse with friends money seems to be no object. A downright noble soul indeed, one of a thousand."

To this compliment Hak Tak made reply, "You flatter me; I do not put forward any such pretensions."

Pettyman then chimed in: "To find a flaw in you would be hard indeed; but your younger brother's disposition is the opposite of yours. Not that we have anything to complain of in his treatment of us, but in his demeanour towards you he is freezing, stolid, lacking in kindness. Does not the elder brother step into the dead father's place? and to be unwilling to show deference to an elder brother is at variance with all orthodoxy."

"I cannot explain this distance between us," said the host. "I neither swear at him, nor use my right to punch; and yet, old tortoise-egg that he is, he treats me as if he had very little care for me."

"I have an idea," Cash broke in, "he suspects you

of using your position as an elder brother to defraud him of his due."

"In what way is it possible for me to defraud him?" asked Hak Tak. "At the most, when friends come to call on us, there is a little additional outlay for eating and drinking from the common purse."

Cash replied: "It is not in these things he mistrusts you, but he suspects you are putting into your own private purse revenue out of your father's estate. That is how matters stand."

Hak Tak exclaimed, with much solemnity of manner, "My conscience is as clear as the blue sky, which fact you, my friends, know very well."

"We, of course, know it," Pettyman said, "but your brother does not."

"The topic is painful," whined Hak Tak. "It is such things which tempt one to say friends are better than brothers."

Cash and Pettyman then feigned the part of virtuous counsellors, and exhorted him, saying: "Well, comrade, do not vex yourself. If your brother misunderstands you, be patient, and do not let him see any outward sign of anger. But to refer to these delicate matters at all is too much like sowing strife in the family. We only spoke because your affection for us seemed to warrant our dropping a word and trying to appreciate your position."

After this interview, Hak Tak felt an unconquerable recoil from his younger brother. He would swear at him whenever a word was spoken that jarred upon his own tastes, and beat him violently whenever anything was done in which his own views were not entirely anticipated.

A Curtain Lecture.

One night, after Hak Tak and his wife had retired, the wife ventured to remonstrate, saying: "My father-in-law had only two sons, your brother and yourself. Can there be the same affection between mere acquaintances as between brethren by birth? How is it that you seem to hate with intense bitterness the sight of your brother? Have not those of our own flesh and blood an equal claim with mere companions? You behave generously enough to those who are only friends, and why should you treat unkindly the son of your own mother? This is loving the distant and slighting the near, looking to that which is outside and forgetting that which is central."

"Be quiet with you. Men of his sort are useless in the world. They are not fit stuff for any kind of work."

To which the wife made retort: "If it be true that your brother is utterly useless, are those two companions so very exemplary and serviceable?"

"How can I do otherwise than take pleasure in their company, when they have said over and over again that in my cause they would dive into the depths, or puddle mud-walls, or even die for me?"

KINSHIP AND KINDNESS

"As to dying for you, that boast remains to be proved; but in my view, whilst friends are for social fellowship, brothers are for love. These men, if I measure things aright, simply hanker after your meat and drink, and I have my fears they may yet drag you under the stream," said the wife.

"What can women know about such things? It is as much as you can do to pick out the different qualities of pomatum with which you smear your hair. No man with a proper sense of dignity will listen to the crude babble of his wife. The reins are in my hands, and it is not for you to be prating on in this style unchecked!" exclaimed Hak Tak.

"Women there may be who concoct scandal and make it the staple of their curtain lectures, and breed schisms between kith and kin; and some men too are nose-led by such wives. For my part, I am only seeking to promote a proper understanding between you and your younger brother. Husband though you are, you can surely heed a sentence or two from my lips now and again. Alas that I am mated to such a stiff-necked man!"

Hak Tak stormed. "My brother is a worthless fellow, and of course I cannot pretend to care for him. How is it that you are so greatly enamoured?"

The wife could only sigh and hold her peace.

It was not long after this conversation that Hak

Tak drove his brother out of doors. Tsun Tak then went to a neighbouring village, and got employment as cook in a rice and wine shop. Cash and Pettyman now had things their own way without any one to check or vex them. Sometimes they would come once in three or five days, and have their banquet of dog's flesh and minced fish, dangling the guitar, smoking opium, and wasting time in games of chance, debauchery, and wine-drinking, till such habits began to tell a tale upon the physique. The wife's tearful remonstrances were all in vain.

A Panic.

One night, after a long carouse in the ancestral temple, Hak Tak came home in a state of partial stupefaction, and his wife said, pointing at him with her finger, "You can think of little else but getting drunk every day."

To this he replied, "If I did not drink, I should have nothing else to do."

"Nothing to do indeed! At last there is something to take up your attention."

The sot angrily entered his chamber and threw himself across the bed. Bending down to his ear, the wife said in a suppressed tone: "Some one has been killed, and the corpse thrown into our back garden. Are you going to drop quietly off to sleep?"

When Hak Tak heard this, he became greatly

alarmed, and his complexion turned quite livid. He could not have been more startled had cold water been suddenly poured down his spine. Smiting the planks of his couch, he asked, "Who is the murderer?" To which his wife replied, "I do not know." "And who the victim?" To which the same answer was returned. Hak Tak then said, "Lead me to the spot and let me see for myself."

With nervous and hurried step he followed his wife into the garden. It was about the time for lighting the lamps, and the night was beginning to darken. There, prostrate upon the earth, lay, sure enough, a lifeless form. The face was difficult to distinguish, but white trousers soaked in blood shrouded the legs.

Hak Tak had all along been a man of somewhat scanty courage. The first glimpse was terrifying, and all the heart went out of him. Ruefully shaking his head, he exclaimed: "We are fated to ruin. I have no idea who can have laid this deep plot against our lives."

His wife replied: "I do not know all the people with whom you may have had quarrels. You must have exasperated some one, who has brought this body here so as to cast upon us the suspicion of complicity in a murder, and involve us at the very least in a heavy money fine."

Hak Tak asked, "Whatever must we do?"

"You must, of course," said she, "get the body buried at once before the thing is bruited abroad. If you succeed in that, you may perhaps escape without further trouble."

"Had we not better hire a coolie to assist us in the affair?"

The wife shrewdly observed: "In a crisis of this sort a hireling is not to be lightly trusted. Our secret might be betrayed, and then endless complications and embarrassments would arise. A matter of this kind can only be confided to bosom friends."

After musing for a minute or two, Hak Tak brightened up and declared, "I have hit upon a scheme that will help us out of our troubles."

Unstable Friends.

Taking a lighted lantern in his hand, he posted away to the house of his friend Pettyman, who, upon hearing his voice at the door, asked him to enter and be seated. Pettyman, smiling, enquired, "What happy fortune brings you here so late at night?"

Hak Tak, taking Pettyman by the hand, led him outside, and said in a subdued tone: "To-night such and such things have befallen us. I want you to play the friend, and give a helping hand in burying the corpse."

But, lo! when Pettyman suddenly heard all this, he thought within himself: This is a matter in which life may be at stake. If any after-accusation arise, I may be found to have brought myself within reach of capital punishment. He then went on to say:

"Old friend, your treatment of me hitherto has been most handsome. If the matter of which you have just spoken had been of another complexion, I could have died for you. But all my life long I have had a dread of looking upon corpses, and at the very mention of such things all sort of fancies start up within me. At the deaths of my father and mother, some little time back, I had to hire people to do the last offices of affection for them, and did not venture even to the coffin side to take a farewell glance. My heart grew sick within me when you just now opened your lips on this matter. Cash has any amount of courage, and I have no doubt it will be all right if you ask him."

Hak Tak then hurried away to see Mr. Cash, and upon reaching his threshold, almost battered down the door in his impatience. Cash enquired: "What is the matter? Why this agitation? Be seated, please. Be seated."

To these introductory courtesies he replied: "I have no leisure to be seated. I just want a word with you."

"What have you to discuss?" asked the expectant friend. "Something good I will wager."

Taking Cash into a quiet corner, Hak Tak told him all about the dead body put into his back garden. When Cash heard it, he said, "Well, what a conscience a man must have, to so plot against the innocent!"

Hak Tak then went on to say, "Pettyman excuses

himself, and I want you to come and give me a helping hand at this critical turn."

Cash reflected that imperial justice undertakes to deal with these questions of life and death, and legal proceedings are sure to grow out of this affair. If Pettyman declines to meddle in this risky business, shall I be stupid enough to have a hand in it? After inwardly musing, he replied : " I, old friend, have no fear of the dead. I could roll corpses about like bamboo shoots, and have no misgivings or heart-quakes. But to-day I unfortunately chance to be suffering from a bad attack of fever. My system is quite unhinged, and I have not been able to eat rice. I was just on the point of calling in my wife to scarify my flesh as a counter-irritant. How is it possible for me to comply with your request?"

"In a case of such extreme urgency," blurted Hak Tak, "you might put a little pressure on yourself and help me."

Cash curtly retorted: "Why need we multiply words over the matter? When in the past you invited me to your table, I accepted the invitations; and now you just ask me to lift up my hand a little, why should I make any ado about it if I could possibly comply with your wish? But I cannot hold myself up a minute longer. I must go back to bed and husband what little strength I have left."

And so Hak Tak, vexed in mind and with falling spirits, had to return crestfallen to his home. The night was gusty, and the wind blew out his lantern, and he several times bruised and skinned his toes, and fell into ugly pitfalls.

Upon his return the wife asked, "Have you secured the help of your friends?"

He replied: "Such a run of checks and mischances is quite unheard of. One of them says he dare not look upon a corpse, and the other has been laid low with a sharp attack of fever."

THE FRIEND IN NEED.

After a pause for reflection, Mrs. Hak Tak ventured to suggest a fresh idea. "Might it not be well if you were to go and see your younger brother? Possibly he might help you."

"Right. Perfectly right. That is a capital idea," said Hak Tak. Having bound up his wounded toes, and relit the candle of his lantern, he trotted away on his new enterprise, and tapped at the door of the shop where his brother was employed.

The master asked, "What grave business can have arisen to bring you here for your brother at this late hour of the night?"

"His sister-in-law has been seized with sudden sickness," Hak Tak replied, "and I want him to go and buy medicine."

"Very good," said the master. "If brothers are not available at such times, what reason is there for the existence of the relationship at all?"

The pair of brothers were no sooner outside the

door than the younger, who was dutifully following in the rear, enquired, " Elder brother, is my sister-in-law in great suffering?"

"It is not that which is troubling us at all," Hak Tak answered; "but some unknown adversary has put a mutilated body in our back garden. I want you to come home and give me a hand in carrying it away, and removing all traces of the crime."

Tsun Tak promptly consented. "Of course I will render this service, for it is only my natural duty."

Upon reaching home, they found the wife had got a rain-cape of dried leaves and some rolls of matting, and had packed up the body into a neat and portable burden. Having raised the grim parcel from the ground, lashed it to a bamboo pole, and placed the ends of the pole on their shoulders, the two brothers fetched a compass round the little hill at the back of the village, with pick and spade in hand. On they tramped, without whisper or sound or rustle, till at length they reached a dark, solitary place at the foot of the mountains, wet and marshy with the recent rains. Here they delved with might and main, and, having reached a depth of about three feet, lowered the corpse into the hole and filled in the earth. Returning home, they tried to pass what was still left of the night in sleep.

As soon as the elder brother had stretched himself out in bed, his heart began to beat with startling violence, and he was haunted with distressing fears. His wife tried to comfort him by reminding him that the night had been dark, and nobody would be likely to have seen the secret funeral. The difficulty had been adroitly encountered, and further forebodings were foolish. Hak Tak could only ejaculate, "May heaven defend us!"

THE CURTAIN LECTURE (*continued*).

After a sufficient pause, the wife gave a new turn to the conversation. "You once observed that Cash and Pettyman would be ready to die for you. What view of the case do you take now?"

The husband parried the question by saying: "Please do not revive that subject. Regret at the mistaken view I took will not undo what is already done."

But his wife persisted. "You once said your younger brother was worthless, not fit material to make up into any kind of useful article. Possibly you see now that he is ever so much better than your friends."

Hak Tak assented. "The saying that the sincerity of kindness is best proved in trouble is abundantly true. It was a maxim of the ancients, 'In the tiger hunt keep by the side of your own brother, and in battle belong to the regiment in which fathers and sons are fighting together.' Nothing could be truer than that maxim."

The wife then asked, "Is not the hair of some women worth softening with good pomatum?"

Hak Tak could not help smiling as he replied:

"Not only does it deserve good pomatum, but golden hair-pins as well. The gayest red petticoat would not be out of place on you. The dressy creatures of fashion are not to be named on the same day with one who knows the art of making peace between kith and kin. I did not think you were such an accomplished physiognomist, and could detect at once the worthlessness of those two acquaintances. You are one of a thousand."

"Friendships are not, of course, to be cultivated without more or less of hospitality," replied the wife, "but to make eating and drinking the one watchword of all social intercourse is to degrade it. Those rogues grew lavish in their expressions of endearment when food and drink were in sight, but their ordinary discourse was like fetid water running out of a rotten pumpkin. I long feared they would corrupt your character and land you in interminable tribulations. Since the time of your first intimacy with them you have grown reckless in your habits. Whenever there was any sight-seeing within reach, those two men would turn up, and one would say, 'We have already hired a boat,' and the other chime in, 'It is anchored just at hand'; and you would dance about in frantic glee, and hurriedly roll bed and baggage together, and be off to spend five or ten days from home in gambling, opium-smoking, and every kind of profligacy. Whilst leading a life of that sort, you could not expect to put on flesh. Too much have you been presuming upon the prosperity of your forefathers. Your parents exercised the most careful economy to get together a little property for their two sons and their descendants after them, and if you squander it uselessly, how will you be able to face your parents in the next world? And whilst you do such things you cannot confront your younger brother here with a clear conscience. Under the influence of those two muck-rake fellows you were fast becoming cruel-hearted and insane."

After the wife had delivered her soul, Hak Tak nodded his head and sighed, adding: "Well, you need not refer to the subject again. I was entirely in the wrong, and see things more clearly now. I will never be cordial with those two men again."

Husband and wife then dosed quietly off till the day broke. No sign of trouble appearing on the morning sky, Mrs. Hak Tak killed a chicken, and bought sundry viands, and presented offerings to the household gods. After these rites, the two brothers and the wife sat down to feast together. In the course of the meal, Hak Tak broke the silence.

"Strange planetary conjunctions have been taking place over our heads, and an unexpected crisis has come; but through the protecting power of the ancestral spirits our troubles are over-past. Hereafter, younger brother, you must not undertake outside employment. You can stay at home and oversee the work of the farm. I see how mistaken I have been in much of my past conduct. In the future I will give more heed to your advice."

"I have no pretensions to virtue," Tsun Tak answered. "If I come home, I will simply do my best."

After giving due notice to his employer, the younger brother returned to take up his old place in the house of his fathers. He was now more prized than gold or jewels. The two brothers ate and drank together with the keenest relish for each other's society, and the face of Mrs. Hak Tak had a new brightness about it, for she was able to dismiss the grief she had long been nursing in her heart.

Coldness between Friends.

Some little time after this incident, Pettyman again presented himself, his face corrugated with insinuating smiles, and said, as though nothing had occurred in the interval, "Well, old friend, you have been having pleasant times of it lately, I suppose."

Hak Tak had little heart for talk, and said somewhat curtly: "Be seated, please. Have a pipe. Take a sip of tea." But he did not emphasise these automatic civilities by rising to greet him. After a short interval, he said to Pettyman, "Keep your seat, but I must be going out to water the vegetables."

Pettyman, seeing plainly that his company had become insipid, turned on his heel and walked away.

In the course of the next few days, Cash also came to call on his former friend and patron; but Hak Tak did not receive him with any more cordiality than the other comrade, and he soon took his departure.

Whilst this slight was still fresh in his mind, Pettyman went to the market-town, and, seeing Cash in the distance, beckoned to him. "Let us go to a tea-shop and sip a cup together." Having entered the shop and seated themselves at a table, Pettyman said in a suppressed tone: "Old friend, how unapproachable that man has become! I went to see him the other day, and he could not well have made himself more stiff and frigid. Indeed, he was scarcely civil and had not the grace to offer me even a cup of water. He has conceived an antipathy for some reason or other, and is simply beside himself with spite."

To which Cash rejoined: "I also called a few days ago, and had precisely the same experience. For some time I have foreseen that he would prove a niggard and a heartless turncoat. Out of respect to the past, however, we perhaps ought not to set ourselves against him all at once. Possibly he feels some offence, because of the night when we were unwilling to help him, and secretly resents our caution. It would have been an omen of ruin for us to look on that dead fellow in his garden. Who would be so stupid as to take a tornado on his own head and dandle it?"

"I at once declined," said Pettyman, "for the same reason. It might have implicated us in an accusation of murder that only concerned himself."

"In the course of a day or two we will go and visit him again," Cash replied. "If he is respectful, and shows us a reasonable degree of politeness, we will let bygones be bygones. If he is intractable as in the past, we will open a well of refreshment for some one out of his entanglements."

Having thus agreed together and made ready their plans, in the course of the next few days, they paid another call upon the lukewarm friend, and, to their mortification, were received with just as much coolness as before. Hak Tak simply asked them to be seated, drink tea, and smoke a pipe, but without offering any further attentions, all the while rattling his *abacus* and taking up his pencil to scribble down his calculations. The two friends, not entirely relishing this new code of manners, promptly made their excuses and retired.

PLOTS AND ACCUSATIONS.

No sooner were they outside the village, than Cash exclaimed: "When friends come from a distance to pay a call, it is simply an outrage to omit every kind of civility and attention. We must lodge an accusation with the mandarin against Hak Tak, or we shall not be able to allay the torment of our indignation. But in indicting a man for a capital crime, it is necessary first to find the body, so as to have evidence on which to rest the case."

"I congratulate you on the sharpness of your wits," Pettyman replied. "No wonder that a village comprising three important clans should have chosen you for its adviser and representative."

Having agreed upon their plot, the next day but one, the two men, wearing broad sun-hats and carrying a spade, went forth and made search along the whole line of hills. Of course they made no inspection of old graves, and if there were a new grave heaped very high, they did not look twice at that. A short grave, they inferred, must be the grave of an infant. For three or four days they peered everywhere without getting a clew. They had reasoned within themselves, as there was no river or stream in the immediate neighbourhood, the corpse could not have been pitched in and allowed to float away. At last they came to a dark and secluded place at the foot of the mountain, very damp, and close by a pool of water. Noticing a patch of ground which had been recently disturbed, they enquired of a cowherd in the vicinity how long it was since that particular piece of ground had been meddled with. He replied: "Not very long ago there were no traces there at all. It was on such a day I first noticed the ground had been disturbed."

They next enquired of some peasants in the neighbourhood what family had its burying-place there; and one of them said, "What fools you must be! for whoever would think of burying in such a spot? It might be an agreeable cemetery for ghosts, but no one else would be likely to use it."

The two friends then said to each other: "That is surely the place. There can be no mistake about it."

Forthwith they set to work with their spade, and

scooped down to a depth of two or three feet, where, apparently, they came upon some kind of body. It was wrapped in matting, and inside seemed soft and woolly. They knew for a certainty that now at last they had turned to the right invoice. Pettyman clapped his hands in glad excitement and exclaimed: "We shall have food and drink now. All kinds of precious stones will come to us out of that mine."

As they posted along, talking of their plans, they came across a young beggar, seventeen or eighteen years of age.

Cash was the first to address him. "Greetings to you on your good luck, younger brother!"

The beggar said: "When a fellow has to bear daily hunger and to beg for food, what good luck is there upon which he can be congratulated?"

"Looking studiously at your physiognomy," replied Cash, "I see beaming there the brightness of a coming light. The tide of wealth is just setting in, and I have a fine money-making plan which I can lay before you. Will you follow my directions or not?"

"By what means is the wealth to be made? I hope you will put me up to the knack of it?"

"A rich man has just contrived the death of a travelling merchant," said Cash, "and we are now proposing to lodge an accusation against him. But there is no one to play the part of aggrieved relative and blood-avenger. Will you give yourself out to be the nephew of the murdered man, and we two will act the part of witnesses? The defendant, fearing lest his head should be forfeit to the law, will make handsome terms with you. You need not fear to ask heavy indemnity. You can stretch the mouth of your beggar's wallet just as wide as you like to receive the silver. No meagre doles of coarse rice will you have to put into it then. You will be able to cast aside your alms-bowl, younger brother, and to get good clothes, and dress yourself up to rank with the best, and, glittering in gaiety, will go back to your native village, purchase a house, marry a wife, and fill the *rôle* of rich man. All that kind of thing is quite feasible."

The beggar smiled and answered: "It would be very grand if it could only be carried out; but I never had an uncle who can be assumed in this case to be the corpse."

"What a simpleton you are!" broke in Pettyman. "It is not necessary for you to have had an actual uncle. We will undertake all such difficulties in the case. The only thing you need is to get ready your money-bags. We are not going to deceive you."

The beggar at last was persuaded to fall in with the scheme, and agreed to follow out their instructions.

Cash then prepared under the signature of the aforesaid beggar a formal accusation charging Hak Tak with the malicious murder of the petitioner's uncle, to which crime Cash and Pettyman were witnesses. The accusation was lodged with the mandarin, who immediately issued a warrant for the arrest of the suspected murderer.

The Trial.

In due time the county commissioner came to hold an inquest on the body and directed that the coffin should be dug up and opened in his presence. When this official had arrived at the foot of the mountain, and was seated in the midst of his retinue, he made various enquiries of the neighbouring inhabitants, all of whom were quite ignorant of the crime. At this point in the trial Mrs. Hak Tak came rushing upon the scene. After paying her respects to the commissioner by falling upon her knees and bumping her forehead nine times upon the ground, she went on to say: "The defendant is the husband of the woman who now addresses you, and has hitherto been a respectable and law-abiding farmer. Of any such crime as murder he has never been guilty. I entreat your honour to discharge him, lest you should unwittingly do a grievous injustice."

The mandarin replied: "The relative of the murdered man who asks for vengeance is here, and by his side stand the two witnesses in the case. Evidence also from the opened grave will by-and-by be produced. How can you expect to deceive me by this disavowal?"

"It was a big dog we killed at our house and

afterwards buried, for it was a custom of the ancients to bury their dogs. If you suspect my story is a fabrication, you can open the grave and see for yourself," answered Mrs. Hak Tak.

The commissioner then ordered a gravedigger to take up the body, which indeed turned out to be a

great dog with a cooking-pot placed for a skull, a quilted jacket round the body, and a pair of white cotton trousers drawn over the hind legs. To make the weight equal to that of a man's body, here and there inside the matting brick-ends had been placed.

The commissioner then said, "That a dog has

died there can be no doubt; but why should it have been gashed after that fashion?"

"Great officer, there is an element in the question of which you at present are in ignorance. Allow me to explain. My husband was once a friend of these two men, Cash and Pettyman—that is to say, they drank a great deal of tea and wine together. These two loafers led away my good man into gambling, extravagance, and debauchery, besides fostering dissensions between him and his own flesh and blood. At their instigation he took offence at his younger brother and turned him out of doors to earn his own living. My husband was deaf to my exhortations. Your mean handmaid could think of no other plan for bringing him to his senses, so she took a big dog, and, having cut its throat, dressed it up like a human figure. At this point in the proceedings, Hak Tak came home half-drunk. It was twilight, and I led him into the back garden to look upon the spectacle; but my good man's courage is rather small, and at the first glance he took the thing to be real, inferring, of course, that some one had put a dead body there to bring trouble on the family. Thinking it was necessary for our safety to secretly bury the body at once, he went to beg the assistance of these two friends, who had often professed their readiness to serve him. Not a step would they move to help him out of his difficulties. He then went and asked the aid of his younger brother, whom he had formerly thrust out from the family circle. The younger brother came at once, which naturally led to their reconciliation. After this my husband became fully convinced that his two comrades were insincere, and coldness arose between them. To spite him for withdrawing his friendship from them, the two men have brought this false accusation. I hope the great officer will punish them heavily for their intrigue. Do not let them slip away like fish through a torn net."

The commissioner then asked Cash and Pettyman if they had once been friends with Hak Tak, and enjoyed his confidence. They replied, "We were thrown together now and again by circumstances, but were not very intimate."

Pointing with his finger, Hak Tak shouted: "Was it indeed only a passing acquaintance between us? The scales scraped from the fish cooked to entertain you when you visited me would fill a hamper, and the feathers of the poultry plucked would scale well-nigh a hundredweight. How can you think of asserting the friendship was only casual?"

The commissioner then interposed. "If Hak Tak did not regard you as confidential friends, he certainly would not have gone in the dead of night to ask your assistance in such a matter. Supposing you had been reluctant to help him in his extremity, there was no need for you to conceive this crafty method of landing him in trouble by a false accusation. Confess what motive led you to act in this way, or you shall be beaten to death with clubs."

The men seemed unwilling to admit their offence, and the commissioner shouted out, "Bring the press boards." At this the two men were so terrified that the perspiration started from their foreheads. Cash wanted Pettyman to speak first, but Pettyman tried to put it upon Cash. The commissioner cut short the controversy by giving the order, "Strike."

Just as the tormentor was getting his hand ready, both men dropped on their knees to the earth and knocked the ground wildly with their foreheads. Cash at length broke the silence by saying: "We admit the past friendship, and concocted this charge to revenge the coldness he manifested towards us after we had refused to help him. We know how wrong it was, and hope your worship will extend to us clemency and forgiveness."

The commissioner broke out in great wrath: "Mean, crafty plotters! The palate is the sole standard by which you reckon things, and you have forgotten the very existence of a conscience. According to the statute book you ought to die by the sword; but I will consent to give you a little grace, and leave you still in possession of your lives."

He then called the lictors, and told them to take the pair of plotters and give them two hundred blows with the large flat boards and two hundred blows with the scourge of split rattans. They beat till the skin was torn, the flesh broken, and the blood ran together in streams. The men cried piteously under the operation, waving their hands and kicking their feet as though demented. After the beating was over, the sufferers rolled from side to side and head to foot, and could scarcely lift themselves from the ground. The commissioner then commanded that Cash and Pettyman should be led to the front gate of the magistracy and be made to sit in the stocks for five months. He next dealt with the beggar.

"You say that you have been bereaved of your uncle, and it appears the only uncle you ever had was a big dog."

"It is quite true I have no uncle," the beggar replied; "but these two men directed me to come to your court and say that I had, and make a pretence of weeping."

The commissioner said: "If they were to bid you die, should you do it? You are young in years, and have been led astray. I will halve the penalty." He then gave sentence of a hundred blows of each kind upon the beggar. Upon hearing which, the beggar beat his forehead upon the earth and said, "Great officer, do not punish so much."

"It is unnecessary to add further words," the commissioner replied. "Inflict the number I have named."

The lictors then laid on till the spirit of the beggar left the body and he had cried himself quite dumb. After the beating he also was led away to be pilloried for five months before the chief entrance to the magistracy.

At the close of the trial the commissioner praised

Mrs. Hak Tak, saying: "This wife has at least seven of the ten qualities which go to the making of a heroine. Skilful in resource, wise to recover her husband to reasonableness and bring about peace between brethren, she is one of the most worthy women on whom the sun shines. I shall present her with twenty dollars from the county exchequer, so that she may go home and feast merrily with her friends and kinsfolk, and stimulate other wives to follow her virtuous example." When he had said this, Hak Tak and his wife touched the ground with their foreheads, thanked him, and took their departure.

As the three men sat pilloried before the front door of the magistracy, the beggar reproached Cash and Pettyman, saying: "You are pretty fellows to introduce one to ways of getting wealth. You simply invented a beating to death for me and a resurrection to bone-aches. It is really more than human nature can stand."

"Of course you find it hard to bear," Cash replied; "but do you suppose it is so very easy for us? You were the accuser and we were only witnesses, and we have been beaten more than you. Of what inordinately hard treatment have you to complain?"

The beggar retorted: "Although you have just been beaten, yet before that you got many a full stomach and many a genial drinking bout. But it has been in your interests that I have personated the aggrieved relative, and all I have got is anguish greater than I can bear."

Pettyman said: "Cash undertook to be the lawyer and conduct the case. If you complain to him, the thing will be put in its proper light."

Cash answered: "Alas! alas! no mortal mind could have foreseen the turn things would take. That this woman should have had hidden in her heart skill for such deep counter-moves baffles all prognostication. Our lives were nearly forfeit to her hand. Lucky was it we did not die."

When Cash and Pettyman had finished out their sentence, they were, as a matter of course, everywhere feared, hated, and despised. No one would have even a speaking acquaintance with them, or invite them to a meal. The two men after a time became sick, and their wives and children died. In the end they were reduced to beggary, and, having spent ten years scouring the country asking for alms, perished of privation.

This crisis in his affairs led Hak Tak to acknowledge the discretion of his wife. He took her hereafter into all his counsels and paid good heed to her advice. The children and grandchildren of this shrewd woman all prospered, one son who opened a depôt for foreign goods in the city of Canton becoming a millionaire. His success was due in no small degree to the sterling worth of his mother.

CHAPTER III

THE GOOD GRADUATE—A LESSON IN CONCILIATION

Tsang Kung Ü.—Father and grandfather of men described in story.
  Son by first wife—A Shing.
  Sons by second wife—A Hau (Filial), A Chung (Faithful), A Sun (Veracious).
  Sons by concubine—A Tai (Brotherly), A Yan (Humane), A Yee (Upright).
Children of A Hau—
  By first wife—Kai Ip (Estate Heir), Kai Tak (Virtue Heir).
  Son by second wife—Kai Kung (Merit Heir).
  Son by concubine—Kai Tso (Ancestors' Heir).

IN the disturbances which occurred before the authority of the Ming dynasty was firmly established, A Shing, the son of Tsang Kung Ü, together with his mother, was carried off by bandits, and was never heard of again during his father's lifetime. To fill up the gap caused by the capture and detention of his first wife and the supposed loss of his only son, Kung Ü married a second wife, who bore three sons, to whom he gave names borrowed from the cardinal virtues, A Hau, A Chung, A Sun, hoping, doubtless, that they would in due time prove themselves models of Filial Piety, Faithfulness, and Veracity. The offspring with which he was favoured through his second wife did not seem an adequate compensation for the loss sustained at the hands of the bandits, or a sufficient insurance in such an unsettled age against the possibility of being left without descendants. He therefore introduced a concubine into his establishment, who in due time bore him three additional sons, to whom he gave names scarcely inferior to those of the first three in their euphonious hopefulness, A Tai, A Yan, A Yee,—doubtless expecting that with Fraternity, Benevolence, and Righteousness added to his household pantheon, his descendants would be honoured for their excellences through many generations. A Tai, the eldest son of the concubine, is the hero of this simple family history.

Funeral Squabbles.

After some years the father of these young men died, and they met to celebrate his funeral, the only absent one being A Shing, who was still in the hands of his captors. As they were about to place the dead body in the coffin, tears started from its closed eyes as from a living spring, at which omen they were greatly alarmed. A Tai, who was a Bachelor of Arts, observed: "Some unlucky event is indicated by these tears which our dead father sheds as he is being put into the coffin. He knows that we lads have been accustomed to bicker with each other, and is not at rest in death because he sees that trouble will come of our fractiousness. These tears now flow to admonish us. We must learn to be conciliatory and forbearing with each other, and must maintain family harmony, so that the spirit of our father may not be disquieted in the under-world." At this piece of advice the other brothers jeered and said, "This weird omen is only because the astrologer we employed did not choose a lucky date for the ceremony."

When the funeral was over, the brothers divided the estate and lived apart. The head brother of the group by the second wife scarcely looked upon the others as blood relations at all, because they had been born of a concubine. He encouraged his own brothers to join him in forming a clique, saying, "We are children of the proper wife, and they of a less regular alliance; and if we should even spurn and cudgel them, they will have no redress against us." The younger members of the trio agreed, following the lead of their elder brother, after the fashion of the fox clothing itself with the tiger's majestic ferocity or the jackal trotting at the panther's tail. Little by little the breach widened. Sometimes the first trio of brothers would feast their friends, and, if the other brothers happened to pass at the foot of the hall, they would take no notice of them whatever, although etiquette would require them to salute an ordinary acquaintance and extend to him a formal invitation to join them at a cup of wine. The two younger brothers of the second trio wished to form a combination of their own by way of reprisal, trusting to the influence of their graduate brother to compensate the inferiority of their birth on the mother's side, and expecting that his prestige would be used to back them in any difficulty created by their independent temper. But A Tai, the good graduate, strongly dissuaded them from any such course, reminding them that if they met a stranger on the road, they would yield to him a step or two, and should therefore be prepared to concede a little on the higher ground of blood relationship.

The Death of A Hau's Daughter— and a Clan Feud.

As time went on, A Hau, the oldest of the first group of brothers, had a daughter, who, when she had grown up to maidenhood, was given in marriage to a member of the Chau family, in the suburbs of the district city. The bride soon died, and A Hau set himself to slander the Chau family, saying the death had come to pass through the failure of the Chaus to provide proper medical attention for his daughter. As in all such calamities, the mother-in-law was singled out for especial blame. Calling together his own brothers and the young hot-bloods of the family, he prepared to have his revenge by sending them to beat his late daughter's mother-in-law. He said also to his half-brother, A Tai: "As you are a graduate, you should have a little more courage than the rest of us. You will have to act with us, and let there be no shillyshallying in the matter."

The good graduate remonstrated, saying: "Your late daughter's mother-in-law could not be altogether without care for her. The physician they engaged found the case beyond his skill, and nothing can be done now to amend the loss. Why try to take revenge upon the mother-in-law? Moreover, if you carry out all that you propose in the way of abusing her, you will still have accounts to settle with her fellow villagers. However importunately you call me to take part in the demonstration, I am strongly resolved to have nothing to do with it."

"Of course you need not go, younger brother. I had thought that as you were a graduate, you would have aided and abetted us with your influence, but you are a good-for-nothing fool, and the education you have received has been thrown away on you."

Giving no heed to A Tai's advice, A Hau went and called together his brothers and half-brothers, sons and nephews, and all the riff-raff of the clan, and sent them to the house of the Chaus, where they seized the old mistress, and thumped and kicked her ferociously. Some of the party went and broke the water-jars, others prized open the rice-locker, others smashed the iron cooking-vessels, others got possession of hatchets and hewed down the front door, and yet others seized bamboo poles and cleared the roof of the tiles, till at last nothing but ruin was left behind. They then went home and reported all that was done. A Hau clapped his hands and danced about, saying, "It is quite refreshing to hear of all this."

When the head of the Chau family had returned from some distant place where he had been staying, he was exceedingly angry at what had occurred. Having engaged a writer to put his complaint into official form, he went and presented the charge to the mandarin. The mandarin promptly granted a warrant, and entrusted the execution of it to a band of police. A Hau and his abetters were arrested, put into chains, and dragged off to gaol, like dogs haled to market. They tugged at A Hau till he was livid in the face, and his brow was covered with sweat, and his mouth was evidently framing to call his younger brother to come and save him. But the police shouted in chorus till the earth trembled, and beat him remorselessly, and would not suffer him once to open his lips all the way to the magistracy. The court having opened, the members of the Chau family were there as witnesses, and no flaw or discrepancy revealed itself in their version of the story A Hau had no course left but to lie recklessly, and assert that his kinsfolk had broken up their own furniture for the sake of giving colour to the false charge they wished to prefer. The mandarin grew hot with rage, and, asserting the majesty of his office, sentenced the men, as a preliminary punishment, to a hundred blows each, whilst A Hau, the instigator, was to receive two hundred blows on the lips. They were, moreover, to be detained in prison till a final decision upon their case should be given. The mandarin was moreover displeased because A Tai, who was a Bachelor of Arts, did not use his influence to restrain his brethren from violence, and purposed taking away his literary rank. He had already drafted a despatch recommending the viceroy to carry out this proposal for degrading him from his position. A Tai, hearing of this, was greatly afraid, and went in person to the mandarin's court to beg for clemency. The mandarin, upon making enquiry about his character, however, found it was most correct and exemplary. A Tai then returned home and went to pay his respects to the Chau family, apologising, in the name of his brothers, for the outrage perpetrated upon them. In acknowledgment of this display of good feeling, the Chau family withdrew from the prosecution, and A Hau and his followers were set free from prison and permitted to return home. But A Hau had no regrets for what had been done, and still nursed the spirit of resentment. In speaking of the affair he treated it lightly, saying there was no case against them, and the mandarin was compelled to release him. When A Tai heard this, he said: "Calamity has not yet passed away from us, and yet deeper troubles are before our family. Hereafter, my brothers will be still less amenable to exhortation."

The House of Mourning and the House of Mirth.

Some little time after this affair, the mother of A Tai, who had only the status of a concubine, died, and the first trio of brothers agreed amongst themselves neither to attend the funeral nor to put on mourning. As the mourners were proceeding to the place of burial, A Hau intercepted the coffin, saying that he could not allow a concubine to be buried by the side of his father. Moreover, he railed at A Tai, saying: "What kind of a person was your mother, that you presume she must, forsooth, be placed by the right hand of our father's grave? It will never do. It will never do. You cannot bury here, and must move away as quickly as possible." A Tai then sought a new place of burial, although it was unreasonable that one who had been thought good enough to share his father's couch in life should not be allowed to sleep near him in death.

About a year after this, A Hau's wife died, and A Tai called his two brothers to go with him and pay their respects to the dead. The two brothers remonstrated, and refused to go, on the ground that at the death of their own mother these half-brothers had ignored all the principles of etiquette. A Tai a second time exhorted them, but, making no reply, they walked away; and, seeing they were so obstinate, he went alone to the house of death, where he wept and prostrated himself with every mark of grief. His two brothers went to their house, which was separated only by a single wall from the house of death, and set themselves to wine-drinking and flute-playing.

When A Hau heard what was going on next door, he was indignant, and called his brothers to arm themselves with sticks and go and chastise these inhuman members of the family. A Tai, seeing what was coming, hurried out first to give a timely word of warning, followed at no great distance by A Hau and his company. As soon as he had entered, he gave an admonitory wink with his eye, and A Yan, who was quick to apprehend things, slipped out by a side door. A Yee could not get away in time, but, as he was trying to jump over the wall, A Hau gave him a blow from behind with his staff about the loins, and he fell back to the ground and rolled over A Chung and A Sun also struck him both with sticks and their fists, as though they were frantically beating a drum. But A Tai interposed himself between the strikers and their victim, saying, "Hold, brothers! I think you have beaten enough."

A Hau swore, saying, "A Tai, are you an abetter of your younger brothers?"

To which A Tai replied: "I make no attempt to extenuate their offence. To play the flute and drink wine was contrary to all propriety, but the sin is not one that should be visited with a death penalty. You have already given them a sufficient rebuke; but if you intend to continue this beating, I wish to bear their punishment in my own body."

"And if we do beat you, what redress have you?"

And they began to thump and strike him as though they were teasing cotton, whilst A Tai clasped his hands and respectfully bowed his head.

By this time the neighbourhood was aroused, and many came flowing in with counsels of peace, and the irate trio took their departure. The good graduate then gathered up the sticks his half-brothers had left behind and took them back to their house with many apologies. But A Hau received him ungraciously, saying that he belonged to a bad lot, and ordered him away from the funeral.

A Yee was confined to bed with his injuries, unable to eat or drink and crying out with constant pain, and A Yan prepared a complaint and sent it to the mandarin, telling of the outrage, and stating, moreover, that when their mother died, these half-brothers had refused to wear mourning. The mandarin then ordered the police to arrest the first group of brothers, and also requested the good graduate to appear and act as adviser in this family quarrel. The assailants were terrified, and had to hide in retired places in the day-time, and at night sleep squatting in large water-jars on the house-roof. A Tai was so disfigured by the blows he had received, and his eyes were so black and blue and swollen, that he could not obey the mandarin's order to appear at the court, and had to write a petition, asking to be excused, and praying that the case might be withdrawn. The petition was granted. After this A Tai's brothers grumbled because he would not take their part, saying, every one had a brother but themselves; to which A Tai replied, that was just what he himself was feeling, for when he exhorted his brothers to peace, they paid no heed to his words. As the feeling between the two sets of brothers continued to grow, and he was helpless to allay it, A Tai decided to remove with his wife and family to a village about twelve miles away, called Yee Tong.

Although A Tai had never taken the part of his own brothers in their quarrels with other members of the family, the half-brothers stood more or less in fear of him because of his status as a literary graduate. After his removal, this fear was taken away, and they became more overbearing than ever to those whom they regarded as inferior members of the family. When the work of the day was over, the two half-brothers used to shut themselves up at home and nurse their knees as if they had fled from an invasion of wasps, and in the end took to carrying knives as a precaution against any fresh act of aggression on the part of A Hau and his confederates.

Return of the First-Born.

At this crisis in the affairs of the family, the son who, many years ago, was carried off by banditti, escaped from his captors and returned to his native village, bringing a wife with him. The family estate had long been divided, and, after discussing for three days the predicament in which they were now placed, A Hau and his brothers could agree upon no satisfactory method of meeting the difficulty. A Shing in the meantime was without any means of livelihood. The concubine's sons, however, entertained him right royally in their own house, whilst one of them went off to inform A Tai of the event, who was delighted beyond measure at the return of this long-lost member of the family. A Tai at once hurried away to visit the restored wanderer, and, making a profound bow, asked, " Elder brother, have you got back to us again ? Good ! Good ! And is this person my sister-in-law ? " and, placing his palms together, he made the usual chin-chin. He then proceeded to ask how his mother was ; to which A Shing replied, she had been long dead. That night A Tai defrayed the cost of a sumptuous banquet, and went to invite the first trio of brothers, who one and all refused to come. After the feast was over, the two brothers sat talking over together the events of the last thirty years till well on to midnight.

On the following morning, A Tai said to A Shing: "Elder brother, you need be under no anxiety about the future. I am residing at a distance, and will give my own house here for you and your family to occupy. And as to the little farm, I have leased it at a small rental, as my livelihood is otherwise provided for. I will make the fields over to you by a perpetual lease so that you shall never be under any obligation to restore them."

A Shing, however, replied: "I have my own title to a share of the inheritance, and will not be indebted to you for private favours. Is A Hau intending to act like one of the Southern barbarians, and treat me as if I were a stranger without family rights? If I impeach him in the courts, the course is perfectly plain; or if I take it upon myself to give him a sound beating, that alternative presents no difficulty."

But A Tai earnestly exhorted him: "Elder brother, I pray you to do no such thing. In all affairs we must aim at a peaceable settlement. I was perfectly sincere in my offer of the farm, and it was no empty speech; and if you do not accept it, I shall not come to visit you again."

The younger brothers joined in offering to give up portions of their fields, and pressed A Shing to fall in with the arrangement. A Shing said: "This is an act of pure kindness on your part, my brothers, and I will henceforth say nothing about any grievance I may have felt." From this time A Shing had house to dwell in and fields to cultivate.

A Tai had only just gone back to his home at Yee Tong, when A Hau and his *confrères* presented themselves at the door of the two half-brothers and began to rail at them, saying: "A Shing is the elder brother of all of us, and not your brother exclusively, and our family affairs must be settled by calm and unhurried consultation if the arrangements made are to be sound and lasting. Why need you give yourselves such virtuous airs and act apart? Are you only just and reasonable brothers, and are we children of wickedness?"

A Yan and A Yee kept silence and returned no answer. But A Shing, who heard what was going on, rushed out, saying: "Good heavens! what new fashion is this? I am son and heir, but have been separated from home for many years; and now I have been lucky enough to get back again, you three brethren have never invited me to a meal of rice or given me a night's lodging. I am indebted to the kindness of my three younger brethren for a roof to cover my head and for land to till; and you fellows without any sense of what is right come here to upbraid them. Do you wish to thrust me out of the place, or would you like to beat me?"

As he said this, his anger rose, and, lifting up a heavy stone, he flung it towards A Hau. It struck his body, and he rolled over on the ground, crying out, "Save life, save life!" A Shing, clenching his fists, began to beat him wildly on the back, saying, "I will do for you, I will do for you!"

A Hau's own brothers, who had been trained to military life and were practised athletes, then rushed into the fray. Rolling up sleeves and trousers legs and binding fast their hair, they made ready for a fierce combat. But A Shing, who had been reared from his childhood upwards in the stockade of bandits, was accustomed to fighting; his size, moreover, was beyond the average, and many a man had he slain in his time. After they had fought over ten rounds, A Shing, using the trick of the snake curling up its tail, turned round and made a sudden kick at A Chung, who fell to the earth. He also thrust his foot into the pit of A Sun's stomach, and sent him flying a distance of ten feet or more. Both cried out with one consent: "Elder brother, you may stay your hand. We will now confess that we fear you and salute you as victor." A Shing then shook his fists towards each of them in sight of the neighbours, who had come upon the scene with hubbub and clamour.

A Shing was the first to lodge a complaint with the magistrate. He related the story of his wrongs, and how, upon his return home, his brothers, who were in possession of the estate, refused to give him his portion. The mandarin said: "You have a brother who is a graduate. The first thing is to call him in as an assessor to determine the right and wrong of the case."

A Tai hurried back to his native village and accompanied the police to court, where he presented himself with face wet with tears. He pleaded that his own literary pursuits had unfitted him for practical affairs, and he had failed in the management of his brothers. He wished to leave the decision entirely in the hands of the mandarin, who thereupon directed that the estate should be divided into seven parts, and that each man should take an equal share. The details of the distribution were left in the hands of A Tai.

Reburial of the Concubine.

From this time forward, the two sons of the concubine who continued to reside in the village became very friendly with A Shing. One day they confided to him the circumstances connected with their mother's death, and the shameful way in which A Hau had acted at her funeral. When A Shing heard this story, he declared that these half-brothers were beasts, without natural affection, and announced his purpose to choose a lucky day and have the body taken up and reburied in due style, by the side of her husband.

When the news of this proposed scheme was conveyed to A Tai, he was troubled, and came over to see A Shing and exhort him to let matters rest, and not to revive bygones. A Shing, however, would pay no heed to these counsels of peace; but, calling together the trio of haughty brothers, said to them:

"Your conduct has been odious. When your stepmother died, you would not wear mourning, and you prevented her own sons from burying her by your father's side. What new doctrine is this, pray?"

The brothers did not dare to reply, but dropped their heads like tortoises contracting the neck to bring themselves fully under cover of the shell. A Shing then announced his purpose of exhuming the bones of his step-mother, and reburying them by her consort's side, and insisted further that each of the sons should be present at the ceremony, and should put on mourning. And with the word he snatched a knife from his girdle, and began hacking a tree as an accompaniment to the comment, "If you do not follow out my instructions, it shall be seen whether the hardness of your necks exceeds the sharpness of my knife."

A Hau said, "Certainly, it is our duty to follow."

To which A Shing replied, "You will not only have to follow, but to wear mourning."

"I understand," A Hau answered. "We will put on sackcloth."

On the day of the ceremony, A Hau ducked in his head and bent himself double, and, lest A Shing should say that he had no filial feeling, put spittle on his face to imitate tears. All the bystanders were splitting with laughter at the farce.

When this event was safely over, the brothers continued at peace for a time. A Shing made free use of his physical prowess to assert his position as the head of the family, and did not scruple to bring his fists down, especially upon A Hau, for whom he entertained a peculiar degree of dislike. He was very respectful, however, to A Tai, whose appearance upon the scene always availed to tame down his fierceness.

A Hau's ways of doing things were somewhat different from A Shing's, and before ten days were over, he went to lay his grievances before A Tai. "I am fierce, but he is ten times fiercer. He is constantly shaming and affronting me." A Tai would then exhort him to bear with his elder brother a little, if he found him rash and overbearing. "You yourself have had your faults, and it is not fitting for you to spend all your time in murmuring at the faults of others."

To which A Hau replied: "Well, A Shing need not think it such an extraordinary thing to fill the position of elder brother, for I have had the office before him. He should count himself lucky to get back home at all, and not presume upon his prerogatives. Is it right to submit to it? Although I may have been testy, I have never been in the habit of beating my brothers. If I have now and again chastised any of my juniors in the home, it has always been in harmony with right doctrine. But this elder brother, A Shing, is simply inhuman, and presumes upon his great size and strength, and is always bringing down his fists upon some of us. Now what remedy is there for this state of things?"

"I can suggest a remedy. Be placid and respectful, and you will be able to transform his disposition. You say that he is fierce, but how is it he never beats me?"

"You live at a distance from him, and, moreover, you are so refined and highly educated, that it is scarcely likely he would lay violent hands on one belonging to the gentry."

A Tai reiterated his exhortations, but A Hau was unwilling to pay any attention to them. After a few days A Chung and A Sun came with their stories. These were also soon followed by A Yan and A Yee.

When not far short of a month had elapsed, A Shing himself came to A Tai, saying: "Younger brother, I do not care to fill this post of chief in the family. And yet if I decline there are difficulties in the way. The younger brothers are very careless, and are constantly provoking my wrath, so that I have to govern the family by the law of fisticuffs. But the most troublesome man of the lot is A Hau, and I cannot bear with his airs at all."

"Elder brother," replied A Tai, "it is not well for you to be angry, for how can you expect your juniors to be quite as clear-sighted and sagacious as you yourself? If they are not wise all at once, you must teach them step by step. Dear elder brother, you have no idea how heavy your fists are, and I am always in terror lest you should inflict serious injury upon those who are of your own flesh and blood. I cannot bear the thought that the spirits of our parents, who are in the realms beneath the Nine Fountains, should be disquieted by these things."

When he had said these words, his tears unconsciously began to flow. A Shing sighed and said, "Younger brother, it is not every one who can take pattern by you."

Having talked and had hospitable entertainment, A Shing went back to his village. And then, in the course of a few days, other two brethren came to Yee Tong, with a fresh cause of quarrel; and A Tai, finding that he could bear the interruptions no longer, removed with his family to Sam Pok, a place about thirty miles off, fondly cherishing the hope that he would at last be spared the bruit of these constant complaints and recriminations.

Hereditary Squabbles.

After A Tai's second removal, the authority of A Shing was asserted without any check; but whilst fierce, he was at the same time just, and all the members of the family stood in awe of him. For a time things ran on smoothly, and then every now and again strife arose.

At this time A Hau was about forty-six years of age. He had first married a wife, who bore him two sons; then he took a concubine, who also bore him two sons; and last of all he raised a slave girl to the rank of concubine, by whom he had one son.

The sons who formed the first family he called Kai Ip and Kai Tak, names meaning Estate Heir and Virtue Heir. The two sons comprising the second family he called Kai Kung and Kai Tsik, names meaning Merit Heir and Accumulation Heir. Last of all, there was a son by the slave concubine, whom he called Kai Tso or Heir to the Ancestry.

The fractiousness of the father descended as an inheritance to the children, and the brothers of high degree set themselves against the half-brothers by the concubines. One day Kai Ip said to Kai Tak: "Younger brother, you and I are sons of the chief wife, but the other three are sons of women who rank lower in the household. It is perhaps only proper that we should carry ourselves somewhat stiffly towards them. They will have no appeal against it if we treat them scornfully or even beat them."

The younger brother replied: "Quite right. We will show them no favour, and when they salute us, we will not recognise them."

When Kai Tsik heard this, he said to his brother: "We must not give in to this kind of thing. If they have two pairs of hands we have four arms, and if they brandish the brass whip we will bring out the iron bar. We shall not go to the wall before them."

"Well spoken, Kai Tsik: I have long had the same thought in my own mind. With this in view I some time since bought a knife, which I have hidden under the bed, so that if they should come to beat and abuse, we can strike the first blow."

And thus the children of the different mothers banded themselves together into cliques and coteries. But Kai Tso had no brother of his own, and his mother died years ago, so he was isolated, and much put upon by the rest.

When A Hau saw the unhappy state of feeling which prevailed in his family, he said: " How is it that you are all so hot-blooded and contentious? The older brothers are without affection for the younger, and the younger void of all deference towards the older brothers. And you are split up into parties and factions, and constantly resisting each other and putting each other down. You could not show bitterer hatred if you were avengers dealing with murderers of a father. Although you may not have sprung from the same mother, you owe your life to a common father, and ought to unite with each other, even as hands and feet of the same body co-operate harmoniously. You will by-and-by have children and grandchildren of your own, and what will be the future of the after races if they take pattern by you?"

But the sons all jeered, saying: "We are not copying any outsider's example, but are simply taking pattern by you. How did you get on with your brothers? You were an expert in railing at them, but never reproached yourself for anything."

Upon hearing this, A Hau silently dropped his head, and then, heaving a long sigh, took his departure.

Now and again A Hau's fifth son, by the concubine, would go to visit his mother's relatives, who lived near Sam Pok, and when he was in the neighbourhood he would drop in and see his uncle A Tai. A Tai had three sons, one of whom had already become a Bachelor of Arts, but the other two were much younger in years. Observing, during a visit of three days, the harmony and happiness which prevailed in the household, he had no desire to go back home. But A Tai pressed him to return, saying it would not do for him to permanently stay with them without his father's consent. Returning home for a time, he took counsel with his young wife, and they agreed, after the father's permission had been secured, to go and live under the protection of their uncle. A Tai was delighted to receive them, and made ready apartments, and arranged for Kai Tso to continue his studies in company with his own eldest son. He proved himself quick and industrious, and in due time his uncle engaged a famous coach to prepare him for the examinations.

After the removal of the fifth son to Sam Pok, quarrels broke out amongst the others with increasing violence, and A Hau had to feign deafness to what was going on, and sit apart with a very sad face. One day, Kai Kung's mother, who had only the status of a concubine, had some words with Kai Ip's wife about the spilling of oil or salt. Kai Ip overheard it, and, growing angry, reviled his stepmother, saying: "Why need you put on such airs?

It is not your turn to speak, even when my wife has said her say. You will be getting into mischief by letting your tongue run too fast." These words provoked the step-mother to a fit of crying.

At this point Kai Kung arrived upon the scene, and, waxing angry and turning red at the few words he caught, said: "Probably the words used by my mother were after all of an everyday order, and conveyed no great offence to your wife. Let the thing be plainly stated and without any exaggeration. My mother is not accustomed to overpaint things."

Kai Ip retorted, "It may be, my younger brother, you want to fight with me?"

"Whether I want to fight or not," said Kai Kung, "is a matter I know best myself. But it is not right to revile a woman in the hearing of her own son, and I will not put up with it."

"If you will not put up with it, how then?"

"I will revile you"; to which the retort was given, "But I will not allow you." Kai Kung replied, "Whether you allow it or not, I shall do it."

When they had reached this point in their wrangle, they put themselves into a fighting posture, rolling up their sleeves and trousers, whilst Kai Ip broke out, "Speak no more; we will settle the right of it by fighting"; and Kai Kung answered, "Well, if you will have it so, we will fight."

Kai Kung, feeling that he was getting the worst

of it, slipped aside into his house for a knife, and Kai Ip, guessing his purpose, went into his house, and as he was coming out of the door again, having armed himself with an iron bolt, his brother, who was waylaying him at the threshold, made a lunge with his knife and inflicted a fatal wound in the abdomen. The day happened to be market, and the other brothers were away from home, whilst the neighbours were so accustomed to these family quarrels that they took no notice of the uproar. The heads of the clan were called together in council, and they bound Kai Kung and delivered him over to the authorities. The witnesses were unanimous, and he could not conceal his crime. After receiving several hundred blows, he was put into prison to await his final sentence. The penalty for fratricide is cutting into a thousand pieces; but, as fate would have it, Kai Kung took sick in prison and died, and was brought back home a corpse to be buried.

The widows of these unhappy men did not dwell under the same roof, and one of them used to go to rail at her sister-in-law's door every day. One morning she ventured inside the door, and the other, unable to control her rage, exclaimed: "Your husband is dead, but is mine alive? If you have no husband, I also am a widow. We are quits in our trouble. Why should you come to curse and rail at me?"

Kai Ip's widow answered: "Your husband took away my husband's life, and, blood for blood, I demand it from you again."

THE GOOD GRADUATE

The other said, "Is this kind of talk meant as an incitement to fight?"

To which answer was given, "I have no fear of fighting you"; and, suiting the action to the word, she flourished her fists in the face of her sister-in-law.

The heavier of the two women succeeded in throwing the other to the ground, and, getting astride her body to keep her down, she began tearing out her earrings, and biting her flesh, and madly bruising her with clenched fists. The smaller of the two women, watching her opportunity whilst her assailant was trying to catch her breath, made a snatch at a vegetable-chopper which lay on the table. Aiming a blow which the other was not alert enough to evade, she split open the skull of her sister-in-law, who rolled over upon the ground and almost immediately died. When the survivor realised what she had done, and the terrible consequences which would be sure to follow, she went and straightway committed suicide by jumping head first into a well. Bereft of two sons and two daughters-in-law after this tragic fashion, A Hau went about with downcast face and shame-stricken and sorrowful mien, for he was beginning to see how his own errors of conduct were involving his posterity in crime and disaster.

But one wave of trouble had scarcely died down before another came. The father of the murdered woman brooded over his loss and its humiliations till his anger became past control. He put down the blame to the mismanagement of A Hau's wife, who was the responsible head and ruler of the younger families, saying she had no care for anything but drinking wine. Calling his sons and nephews together, and arming them with brass-tipped whips and iron-shod poles, he led them to the house of A Hau to take vengeance for their family wrong. When they had arrived in groups at the place whither they were going, they suddenly seized A Hau's wife, and, having stripped off her clothes, beat her unmercifully. A great cry was raised, "Save life!" and A Shing appeared upon the scene in great anger, saying, "The deaths in my family are like a heap of tangled hemp, and you come here to put blame upon my stupor?" Calling together his sons and nephews, they came forth armed with knives and sticks, and the first thing they could find, buzzing like swarms of wasps and mosquitoes. The men of the attacking party at once lost courage and took to their heels. A Shing, however, managed to get hold of a man named Tai Lap, and cut off both his ears. Tai Lap's son turned back to rescue his father, but was set upon by Kai Tsik, who broke one of his legs with an iron bar. Almost all the members of the attacking clan received more or less of damage in the scrimmage. Tai Lap, covering up the place of his ears with his hands, and with ashen face, bounded off from the place as though a ghost were at his heels. Tai Lap's son lay on the ground and could not move. A Shing bade some men put him on a bed-board and carry him away, and, laying him down by the side of his own village, come back as promptly as possible. A Shing then directed Kai Tsik to send in a complaint to the district magistrate, describing the attack that had been made upon him, and giving full particulars about his injuries. The other side also preferred their charge, saying they had simply gone to place incense before the grave of one of their own family, and to make enquiries about the circumstances of her death, and this wanton attack had been made upon them. The magistrate was angry, and, sending three bands of police to surround the village before daylight, captured all the members of the family but A Chung, who managed to make good his escape. A Shing and his allies were dragged off to prison, and beaten till the sky faded from their view and the earth became black as a coke. No money was at hand to bribe the lictors, and the members of this contentious family were tied up to the ceiling like so many lanterns hung from the rafters of a temple, and beaten till they were black and blue. They could do nothing to save each other, as the men entrusted with the task of carrying out the penalty took turns, and alternately beat about head, hands, and body quite blindly. The utmost the victims could do was just to turn pitiful looks upon each other.

In the meantime, A Chung, who had escaped capture by the police, went off to Sam Pok to ask for the advice and mediation of A Tai. Upon arriving before the door, he had not courage to enter. Strange to say, as he was standing there, A Tai and his oldest son and nephew, who were just returning from the Triennial Literary Examination, came upon the scene. A Chung fell at his feet and made obeisance. A Tai lifted him up and took him into the house, so that he might tell in detail of the new distress which had overtaken the family. So great was A Tai's terror when he heard the narrative, that great beads of sweat stood upon his brow, and he exclaimed: "If it be thus, what hope can there be of bringing about a satisfactory settlement? They are all violent in temper, and I had a timely forecast of the woes which would come to them. Had their conduct been otherwise, I need not have moved away from them to this distant place. I have had no intercourse with the district magistrate for some time, and if I interceded with him, I should only meet with a rebuff and be put to shame. Should one of us happen to succeed in the examinations from which we have just returned, and should the wounded men on the other side recover, as a matter of special grace we may perhaps be able to get the case taken off the charge list."

A Chung stayed with his half-brother for some days, till it should be seen what course events would take, and was so struck by the peace and delightful affability of the household that he began to see the evil of his past and to desire better things for himself. On the tenth day of the ninth moon the lists of successful graduates were issued in the provincial capital, and A Tai and his sons were bracketed together in first-class honours, whilst the nephew also was found to have earned for himself a very creditable second class. The house was full of rejoicings and congratulations.

In the Ming Dynasty great honour was accorded to successful graduates, and the whole city and its officials united together in showing respect to literati who had won distinction. A Tai went to offer his greetings to the district magistrate, who congratulated him upon the renown he had won, and paid him every possible token of respect. After this, A Tai ventured to speak of the family disgrace, which was such a pain to him, and asked, as an act of special favour to him in his success, that the criminal action might be stopped. The magistrate replied that to dismiss the case was comparatively easy, but they must be bound together to keep the peace henceforth. A Tai then went to the Pang family to apologise for the outrage, and insisted at the same time upon paying all the medical expenses incurred on behalf of the injured. The head of the family was not altogether pleased to let the case drop, but could scarcely resist the kind and dignified appeal of this distinguished graduate. A Shing and his allies were then liberated.

As soon as he met A Tai, he rushed forward, bowed his head to the earth, and offered his congratulations, saying: " Younger brother, high Heaven has eyes to see, and does not overlook your worth. You have always been a peacemaker, and have put up with many a grievance in silence, and now honour comes to you and to all your household. Do not return to live at Sam Pok, but come and make your home amongst us, and teach us, so that we may purge ourselves from the faults of the past, and find escape from those violent tempers which lead men to laugh at us and despise us for mere cattle."

"Well," said A Tai, "it is an easy matter for me to return; but what if my brothers and sons will not listen to counsel?"

"If you do not believe," replied A Shing, "we will meet together in the temple and swear solemnly by the gods to follow your lead from this time forward, and obey your bidding."

A Tai said, "If all our brothers are of one mind in this thing, it will be the beginning of better days for the whole family."

He thereupon moved back to his native village, and was received with not a little festal welcome. A Shing then assembled the members of this group of families, and after fastings and lustrations made them burn incense and announce to the blue heavens a vow "hereafter to repent of their past faults, and put away all resentments, and maintain family harmony and affection, and practise good works, thereby seeking providential blessing." After the declaration had been made, each person of the assembled households had to touch the ground with his forehead in token of adhesion to the terms of the vow. They then gathered in the open court, and A Tai preached to them from time to time upon the importance of the family virtues, illustrating his discourse by examples from antiquity. Mirth and pathos were deftly blended in his addresses.

After he had conducted a fortnight's mission for the revival of the domestic virtues, a great change came over the male and female members of the family alike, and their fierceness all but disappeared. Upon meeting their neighbours, they unconsciously dropped their heads. In a little time the true temper of harmony began to grow up within them, and at length that brightness of face associated with pacific and affable dispositions began to show itself. Many people styled A Tai, M.A., a living idol. His eldest son became a mandarin, and his youngest a graduate of great distinction, and for several generations the succession of brilliant scholars never failed within the family.

CHAPTER IV

THE HAUNTED MELON GARDEN

THE following story will perhaps justify the partiality felt by lovers of the Chinese for Chinese ghosts. They are pre-eminently sensible, and have attained a far higher level of thought and culture than their Anglo-Saxon congeners. To hear how the ghosts of Shakespeare and Milton and Carlyle can maunder and twaddleise at English and American séances adds a new terror to the humiliation of death. Chinese ghosts always maintain the reputation of the race from which they sprang for strict mental sobriety, and make themselves the vehicles of excellent moral precepts. A ghost should always justify its intrusion into human affairs by sound speech that cannot be condemned.

At the time of this incident, Chan A Sz, a native of the Tsong prefecture, was in his twenty-second year. He was a market gardener by trade, and a bachelor through stress of poverty. One night he went out to keep watch in his melon garden. It was the third or fourth day of the fifth month, and a faint shimmer of light fell from the crescent moon. The light brought into view four or five shadowy forms that were strolling under the trees by the hillside. As they talked together in subdued tones, A Sz thought within himself, "The look of these men is scarcely that of melon-stealers." Clutching in his hand a hedge stake, he crept in amongst the thick foliage to conceal himself as he watched their movements.

All at once he heard one of the forms say: "Let us go together into the melon garden for a whiff of the melon flowers, and to watch the little melons as they are rounding into form. What say the rest to the proposal?"

"We must not go upon any consideration," replied a companion. "Mischief will come of it. If we meet Chan A Sz, and he should be frightened to death, the adventure will be disastrous to all concerned."

The rest laughed. "Have you not already died and become a ghost? Do you suppose you might have to die over again? As far as our experience goes, it is men who stand in dread of ghosts. Who ever heard of ghosts being afraid of men? A chicken-hearted kind of creature you are!"

The ghost who had remonstrated against the reckless saunter replied: "If your courage is so great that you have no fear whatever of men, how is it that you never venture upon apparitions under the broad light of noonday?"

Quoth the other: "It is petty and childish in you to contradict after this fashion. Although I may fear men in general, I have no fear about this particular man, Chan A Sz."

In reply to the other ghosts, who pressed him for the reason of his courage in this exceptional case, he said: "A day or two ago I went into the court in which the Guardian Spirit of the Ground presides, and happened to cast my eye upon a despatch from the king of Hades, giving a list of those whose souls were shortly to be required of them. Chan A Sz's name was in the list, and he will have to die within a couple of days. Before long he will be walking a companion with us in the Tartarean shades. What have I to fear, then, if this is already decreed?"

A ghost interposed: "You only just begin to understand the speech and rudiments of ghost life.

You know your *A*, but you do not know your *B* and your *C*. The man will not die yet awhile."

The other ghost chuckled and said: "How is it that you seem to be so far ahead of us in your information? You will perhaps explain yourself."

The ghost claiming superior knowledge answered: "Well, I will tell you. As late as yesterday, I also went into the court of the Guardian Spirit of the Ground, to see the judge. A despatch had just arrived from the Protecting Spirit of the city, saying that Chan A Sz's mother had recently performed a work of very high merit, and in recompense of that work, it had been decreed that twelve years should be added to his life."

One of the ghosts asked, "What was the nature of this particular act?"

The speaker replied: "Within a few doors of Chan A Sz's house there lives a rich old lady, who recently missed two strings of cash, and suspected her slave girl of having stolen them. Day after day she beat the girl, promising that if she would only confess to the offence, there should be nothing more said or done in the matter. If, however, she refused to confess, the mistress avowed she would not cease her blows till she had beaten her to death. The father of the slave girl heard of the affair, and was very angry with his daughter. He declared that if it should be proved she were the culprit, she should be thrown into the river, and forfeit her place amongst the living. The poor slave girl sobbed with little intermission day and night, and every way of escape seemed closed against her. Because of this incident, Chan A Sz's mother was overwhelmed with grief. There seemed to be no evidence to either convict or exculpate the girl, and it was all but certain that she would have to die. In pure pity the mother of this market gardener pawned her clothes and trinkets for about two thousand cash. She took the cash to the rich old lady and said: 'Several days ago I called here and found no one at home. I happened to see a hundred or more strings of cash heaped up on the floor. All at once the passion of covetousness sprang up within me, and I helped myself to two strings, thinking that out of so many you would scarcely miss them. The loss came to your notice, and suspicion fell on this slave girl. I could not be at peace, as you were beating her so terribly. Probably it is because I neglected the improvement and cultivation of my character in some previous state of existence, that I am condemned to poverty in the present life. To the score of wrong-doing already recorded against me, shall I add this sin, which may need to be avenged in yet another cycle of life? I now restore the full tale of cash, and hope you will be magnanimous and forgive my misdemeanour.' The rich lady answered: 'Of course I did not know that it was you who had taken the cash under these particular circumstances. If you had been in straits, there was nothing to prevent you from coming to me for a small loan. Since you have returned the cash, and all is now cleared up, I shall cherish no ill-will. You need not brood over the matter for a moment.'

"When the two had parted, the God of the Furnace (who fills the office of recording angel) reported the meritorious act in heaven, and Yuk Wong reported it to the Protecting Spirit of the city. The Protecting Spirit of the city found, upon turning to his records, that, for the neglect of moral culture in a former life, Chan A Sz's mother was to have an only son, who would maintain her till she was old, and then die, leaving her desolate and solitary for the rest of her days. Bitter and intolerable destiny, it was decreed that Chan A Sz was to die in his twenty-fourth year, on the sixth day of the fifth month. But since the accomplishment of this meritorious act, it had been determined that the life of the son should be lengthened out twelve years, so that he might be able to minister to his mother to the end of her days. You, brother ghost, did not know the affair from beginning to end. No wonder your spirits rose so high, when you were anticipating the pleasure of Chan A Sz's company in the shades of Hades within a night or two."

The other ghost laughed and said : " Ah ! who could have thought that the omens of destiny would change so entirely in a few short days? It is quite within the bounds of rational belief that Yama's edicts may be supplemented and revised, and that nothing of what has been written down in the Book of Fate is entirely unalterable."

When Chan A Sz overheard these words, he unconsciously heaved a deep sigh, and the troop of ghosts suddenly vanished. Fear on the one hand and joy on the other, took possession of the young man's mind. All night long he revolved the incident, and came to the conclusion that good works might lengthen out a life, to which no medicines could add a single span. A Sz had been filled with indignation when he first saw his mother take the two strings of cash and give them to another, but upon hearing this conversation amongst the ghosts, he came to see that the act was to save a fellow creature, and all his indignation melted away. He also reflected within himself, if he had been originally predestined to a very short life, and a virtuous act done by his mother could avail to lengthen out his life for an additional term, what plan should be adopted that would serve him at the end of the twelve years? "My wisest course," he thought, "is to do some good act every day, and at the end of twelve years the sum of merit will be not inconsiderable. The great God may again add something to my life; and if I go on in right paths, my virtues will grow with my growing years, and I shall come to a ripe old age, and have many sons and daughters. My family is poor, and almsgiving is impossible. I call to mind that no virtue is equal to that of filial piety. The supreme merit is attained by an obedient son." It thus became his joy to minister to his mother in her declining life. She attained the age of eighty before she passed away. After this, the market gardener married and had sons. To the very end he was zealous in all good works and died after a tranquil and unclouded old age.

CHAPTER V

THE DASHING WIFE

DURING the reign of the emperor Kin Lung, there lived in the Wan Chau prefecture of the Chit Kong province a farmer named Tsai Chung Leung. His circumstances were fairly prosperous, and he had two sons, the elder named Sz In, and the younger Sz Tak (Meditating Wisdom and Meditating Virtue). The elder, Sz In, who was of quick natural abilities, went away from home in the course of time to engage in business. He was married to a young lady of great attractiveness, whose maiden name was Shan, and to whom he became passionately attached. This charming person entertained her husband with all the arts at her command. Of fair countenance and pleasing address, that three-inch strip of flesh, called the tongue, tripped off perpetual talk with much spice of freshness and romance about it. Sz In esteemed her the chief of pearls, and hung upon all her words. Whenever he visited his native village, he divided his money into two halves, giving one to his parents and the other to his wife, at which apportionment his wife of course was immensely pleased.

One night, as they were talking together in bed, she said to Sz In: "I account myself greatly favoured by fortune, for I have a good husband, am well content, and have nothing to give me anxiety. There is only one thing which now and again disturbs my peace of mind. I fear lest anything should happen to you. If that should come to pass, I should never marry again. It would not be easy to find a husband as good as you."

Sz In laughed and said: "That is true; but you are not alone in the resolution you have formed; I should not marry again if anything were to happen to you, nor would I chafe against my solitary lot. I should know it would be impossible to replace you."

"But it would be much easier for me to carry out my resolution of never marrying a second time than for you, because you have still parents living, and would not be able to settle that matter for yourself."

"If anything were to happen to you, I would never go home again, and my father and mother would have no one upon whom to put pressure but each other."

"In vowing not to go home again you are vowing what is impracticable. You talk untruthfully now."

"What sort of a person do you suppose I make you to be? I might possibly lie to my father and mother, but never to you. To speak one's deepest sentiment, at the outset of life the need of parents is strongly felt, but afterwards the wife becomes the indispensable companion. At my present stage of life parents have become a matter of indifference to me. I can get along either with or without them. But as for my wife, I could not do without her for a single day. I cannot eat my rice with any degree of satisfaction when I come home, till I have first seen your face."

"I also assert," said she, "that an angelic helpmate is more to a man than parents."

Sz In replied: "You are clear-sighted, and I am free from error."

From this time forward husband and wife were just like wax or glue in their attachment to each other.

Mencius said, "In childhood the human instinct inclines towards a parent, but in maturity towards a wife." Tsai Sz In's love for his wife was mere love for her beauty, and his wife's love for her husband was mere love of his money. The heavenly wife had no insight into great principles of duty, and thus she accounted parents as mere refuse to be cast away. Both were ungrateful, and their talk about not marrying again was an idiocy of effusiveness and superb stupidity ill beseeming just husbands and chaste wives, who wish to uphold the normal relationships of life. If a tumour as large as an orange were suddenly to grow on the wife's nose, or her eyeball were to swell to the dimensions of a snail-shell, the pleasing countenance would become repulsive; and it is to be feared Sz In would then dislike her, and cease to give her money, and wish her dead and out of sight, the sooner the better. And it is also to be feared that if Sz In had fallen down, broken a leg, and been unable to walk, or had fractured his arm and been unfit to work, so that poverty would have come in place of abundance, Sz In's wife would have been full of groanings and laments, neglected her duties, and have angrily reproached herself for having made such a mistake in marriage. Love to a husband can only be proved in poverty, and love to a wife when the countenance is more or less repulsive.

When the wife saw how much she had endeared herself to her husband, she put on supercilious airs, spending the money he gave her in fine clothes and gay dressing. To-day she would invite somebody to go with her to worship the idols, and to-morrow perhaps she would sail forth to visit some relative, or have a round of sight-seeing. Whatever whim seized her, she indulged it without check or restraint, and lived her own life at will ; and although her husband's parents exhorted her from time to time, she gave no heed to them whatever.

Some little time after Sz In paid one of his visits home, and his mother said to him : " The family of your parents is but poor, and I hope you will contribute a little to the expenditure necessary for the different members of the household. It is a strain sometimes to buy such daily necessaries as rice and fuel, oil and salt. If you have any surplus cash, why not hand it over to your father, so that he can purchase a little land for you? It is surely not needful to give so much to your wife, who will only be getting into extravagant habits by having too much loose cash at command."

Sz In made no answer, but without any further word went home and said to his wife: "My mother has been bidding me not to give over my money into your hands. She says you are careless in your expenditure and are growing extravagant. I do not know in what particulars you are a spendthrift."

The wife then swore at her mother-in-law some twenty or thirty times, calling her a garrulous dog, who was always stirring up contention. The whole night long she made a pretence of crying, and Sz In had to do his best to quiet her down by saying: "I do not agree with what my mother says, but simply repeated her words. Why need you blame me?"

The wife then said: "Do you suppose I spend money without any thought whatever? An ugly dog is a disgrace to his owner, and if I am not smart in my attire, will not people say Mrs. Tsai Sz In is no credit to her husband? And, moreover, the reason I am always going round to the temples to worship is, because my fate is unhappy. I have been married to you two years without the luck of becoming a mother, and I am hoping for the idols to give me their favour, so that I may soon have a son, for whom

I in due time may obtain a bride, to be with me in the house by the time I am thirty-seven or thirty-eight. You and I may then hope to be patriarchs under our own roof, with children and grandchildren around us, and receive unceasing blessing. Do you want to wait till you are fifty or sixty before you have a son, whose only duty will be to stand at the head of your coffin? You are a man, and know how to make money; but have you no forecasts for the future in the direction I have just hinted?"

Sz In laughed. "I scarcely expected to find you so shrewd and far-seeing, and am not surprised people should credit you with being a clever woman. They are not so far wrong after all."

After Tsai Sz In had gone back to his shop, his wife, thinking herself a person of unusual importance, would scarcely look at her father and mother-in-law. One day her husband's brother, Tsai Sz Tak, came in to address to her a word of exhortation. He was the first to speak. " Sister-in-law, my older brother is away at business, and the money he makes by trade costs him not a little toil. In being so very gay and extravagant, you are, in some slight degree, exceeding your position; my father and mother, moreover, have worked very hard all their days, How can you discharge the obligations which rest upon a wife, if you wander idly about. It will be better for you to be more careful, and stay a little oftener at home."

The woman answered: "You insinuate I am not

careful? Do I throw the door wide open at night before I go to bed? If your parents work hard and are parsimonious, it is their own choice. Who refuses them permission to spend lavishly? You speak of the toils and struggles of your brother in business. I never hear him refer to such things when he comes home. What concern of yours is it if I only use my own money? Should it be that I have married a kind husband, the good luck of that is all my own. How wanting in practical sagacity you must be when you set yourself to manage the trifling affairs of women. Surely you must feel ashamed of yourself."

Sz Tak then said: "My brother is of his father's flesh and blood, and you did not bear him; and children are brought up so that they may watch over the aged. My parents have had very little pleasure in their lives, and you flit to and fro as gay as a fairy."

"Is the lot of your parents, sir, so very unusual? It is through me that you have any money to spend in your household at all. Your brother has already avowed that if I were to die, he would never come home again. And then the entire family would be without a prop to support it."

"No more of this wild and extravagant talk, please. Would my brother be under the necessity of remaining a widower all his days if anything were to happen to you?"

The wife changed colour, grew furious, and exclaimed, "If you do not believe me, I will die, and then you will see for yourself!"

"I am not going to drive you to your death," said Sz Tak. "I simply address a few words of wise exhortation to you,—quite an every-day matter after all. Your husband, of course, is nearer to you than I am; and if you have no care for your husband, die by all means. What concern of mine is it?" Having thus spoken, he went away.

The same night the wife retired to her chamber, not, however, to regret her fault. She only said to herself, "I can embroil and embarrass the whole family by my death." At midnight she hung herself from one of the rafters.

The following day a messenger was sent off to inform her parents of the suicide. In hot haste her father and mother came flying upon the scene, asking in excited tones: "Why has our daughter died? She has certainly been ill used in some way or other. Her husband is not at home, and we must demand the reason from you old people. Be quick and tell us. It will not do for you to refuse information."

Tsai Chung Leung then said to his relatives: "This affair arose out of a trifle. Your daughter was a little reckless in her expenditure, and slovenly in the discharge of domestic duties, and our younger son spoke two or three words of admonition which were very displeasing to her, and she grew angry, and ended life by her own deed. She had no other ground of resentment."

The parents of the poor suicide then said: "According to your own statements, you abetted your younger son in his language. He had clearly taken advantage of his position to vilify his sister-in-law, and, unable to bear the shame, she put an end to herself. These wrongs and oppressions dishonour all human relationships, and we shall certainly accuse you to the magistrates, and it will be no easy matter for you to get out of the toils."

Shaking with anger, and making the most frantic threats and demonstrations, they went away, saying, as their last word, "We shall now go and engage a lawyer to prepare the accusation, and lodge it at the mandarin's court."

Tsai Chung Leung, seeing that things had reached this serious pass, and, making sure that a false charge would be preferred against him, knew that it would end in litigation, and involve a large expenditure of money. Moreover, he reflected that the character for mandarin is composed in part of the two characters for mouths, and his mouth is big, and my mouth is little. If I say a thing is false, he will say it is true, and endless complications will arise. The best thing will be for us to swallow our anger, and say no more about it, but send an intermediary to negotiate for the withdrawal of the action, upon payment of reasonable compensation. He then engaged a cousin of some little standing and prestige to go and talk matters over with them, but he found them very unwilling to arrest the proceedings. The only terms to which they would listen was that thirty acres of land should be given as indemnity. Tsai Chung

Leung had no alternative left, and was compelled at last to fall in with the proposal. Having written out the deed conveying the field to the new owners, he took his departure.

After the daughter-in-law's funeral was over, the son Sz In came home. It was his duty to speak a few words in the presence of his parents to the effect that the miserable woman after all was one with whom there had been some occasion of revenge in a preceding state of existence, and she had therefore come to harass and distress them for a time in the present life. "But, dear parents," he should have said, "think no more about her. I will seek out a woman of good disposition, marry her, and bring her home to serve you in your old age, and then all will be well."

If, after some such fashion as this, he had comforted the heart of his father and mother, it would only have been in agreement with right doctrine. But, far from adopting any such strain, he did nothing but weep day and night, and would scarcely eat rice, lamenting without ceasing the loss of such an excellent wife.

Tsai Chung Leung uttered an unconscious sigh, and exclaimed: "I have been engaged my whole life in farming, and have had food and raiment, and a fair share of comfort. Never have I had any great sorrow, and could not have dreamed that now my daughter-in-law would have died and my fields have wasted away. Our son, too, has no thought of our trouble, and only adds to the burden of our vexations. What use is life to me? It would be much better to die." In the middle of the night he went out to the fish-pond in the front of the village, jumped in, and drowned himself.

The following morning the old man's wife asked, "Where was your father going that he should need to get up so early?" and all said they did not know. That day no trace or shadow of him was to be seen, and as a matter of course many misgivings arose. They sent men out in every direction to enquire for him, but the search was fruitless. On the second day the body floated to the surface of the pond, and it was then known that he had stepped into the water and died by his own act.

The widow of the second suicide then hurried away to the house of her late daughter-in-law's parents, and cursed them in loud terms, saying: "Your daughter died, not because anyone had beaten her, nor because she had been driven to it by ill usage, but because she wished to shorten her days, and had no love for life. It was not a very tragic affair, but you exaggerated it, and came and terrorised us to such an extent that my husband made a compensation in land to you for your bereavement. It was not of his own free will, and it has so preyed upon his mind that he himself has now died by his own act. It is entirely through you, and I now take an oath that I will not live in the same world with you. We will both travel one way, and then the matter will be at rest." Having thus said, she threw the weight of her body forwards, and clutching the father by the bosom with one hand, and grasping his beard with a death-grip that would not relax in the other, just as though she were lugging a dog along, she screamed without stopping, "We must go into the pool and be drowned together." As she dragged him along, his face grew livid, his breath went away, his lips were unable to frame a word, and his very soul seemed to have left the body. When the bystanders saw the fury of her demeanour, and how unequal they would be to a contest with this frantic creature, they contented themselves with exhorting her, and saying, " Relative, you need not get so very angry; we cannot bring the dead to life again, but we will give you back the field, and we shall then be quits."

The widow of Chung Leung answered: "You may return the land, but will that be sufficient to appease my heart? I do not want it; I simply want to die in his company." She also added, "Get good coffins for us, and the masses for our souls can be said at one function." No heed would she give to remonstrance. When the father of the ill-fated bride saw there was no other way out of it, he wished to give, besides the old field he was restoring, thirty acres of land more. Chung Leung's widow then insisted that the deed should be prepared on the spot, and that the elders should be called in to witness its execution, before she would consent to go home.

The story-teller adds his comment. This woman

was not wrong in demanding back her field, but she was wrong in asking for more than the return of her own. If blood-money were always to be insisted upon, a man with ten bad daughters might get three hundred acres through their suicides, and it would then be no longer necessary to dig the gold mountains in order to become rich.

Tsai Chung Leung's widow having returned home, and observed the funeral obsequies of her husband, the father of Sz In's late wife began, in his turn, to feel resentment, and said: "I have never allowed anyone to cheat me hitherto, and now this blatant woman has annexed thirty acres of my land. I am not at all content to let things stand as they are at present. But if I go and lodge a complaint with the mandarin, the extortion, it must be allowed, began first with our side. On the other hand, it is intolerable to be gagged and quietly to swallow one's grievances." This old gentleman then said to his wife: "I will go to the house of our late daughter's mother-in-law, vile beast that she is, and will hang myself before her door. If you then go and complain to the mandarin, we can involve them in difficulties, the settlement of which will swallow up all that they have."

"Do not make any such mistake," said his wife. "You first committed an act that was ungenerous, and as a reprisal there came on you an act that was unjust; but this was exactly what might have been foreseen. It is a common incident of life. If you use a corpse to shuffle trouble on to others, you will be the first transgressor, and will only make yourself laughed at. Whilst a man is still upon the earth, life is the most important thing for him to consider, and riches must be looked upon as things that may either come or go. No one would think of destroying money for the sake of making ashes, and a life must not be wasted with the view of bringing trouble upon others." The husband was silent, and made no answer to this expostulation; but the wife watched all his movements with great solicitude.

One evening a relative had invited him to a feast, and at midnight there was no sign of his return. His wife then sent a messenger out to make enquiry of the relative where he was feasting, who said, "The old gentleman, after drinking several cups of wine, said, 'I have a pain in my stomach, and must ask to be excused.'"

His wife then sent neighbours to search in the village to which his daughter had once gone as a bride, and, lo! he was found hanging by the neck from above the door of his son-in-law's parents, swaying from side to side, like a dried duck looped up in the wind.

On the morrow this latest widow went to lodge an accusation with the mandarin, and the mandarin arranged to come on a given date, and hold an inquest over the body. The old men who represented the two families gathered together to discuss things, and said: "The parents of the young wife made her suicide an occasion for false accusation and

THE DASHING WIFE 101

money-getting, and then suicide was provoked in the family of the young widower. There was a death and a false accusation in the first case, and a false accusation and a death in the second case. If no bounds can be put to this temper of resentment and extortion, before long there will not be a life left in either family. We have the authority of old age, and ought to arrange these troubles, and end once and for all these recriminations. By encouraging malice are we ourselves to be involved in litigation, and allow the yamen underlings to eat us up bodily? It is only right that the young widower's family should take the thirty acres of land belonging to the Shan family, and restore them to their original owners, and that the family of the young wife who committed suicide should take the dead body and bury it on the hill-top, so that no further trouble may arise out of this affair. A paper, moreover, must be sent in to the mandarin, saying that the differences have been settled, and that there will be no litigation." Upon these terms they were all agreed to settle this tangle of feuds.

THE WIDOWER SEES A GHOST.

In the meantime Tsai Sz In did not reflect upon his fault or repent his early mistake. After going back to his business establishment, he never revisited his home for the space of two years. He did nothing but think upon his wife and lament her death. One night, as he was sitting upon the side of his bed ungirding his clothes before retiring to rest, there came a fierce gust of wind, and the flame of the lamp grew green in hue, and then there appeared two demon torturers from Hades, one hand of each grasping a brazen scourge and the other an iron prong. Between them crouched his former wife, Shan She, chained by the neck, head split open, hair dishevelled, the flesh of her face withered and wasted, and her body scored over with blood-marks. Weeping towards her husband, she said: " Presuming upon my husband's great love to me, I threw away my life; as the result, disasters have fallen upon the parents of the two families. The judge of Hades has therefore sent me down into the Im To purgatory, where I must be tortured for twenty years, and then be twice re-born as a quadruped before I can pass again into a human form. At new and full moon I have to receive one hundred blows from the loaded whip. I was wrong, a thousand times wrong; but now repentance is unavailing. Husband, you have listened to the voice of your wife, and have paid no respect to your parents. Because of your virtue in a preceding stage of existence, you ought to have had three sons born to you, and have made a fortune of many thousands of dollars. But your original destiny of happiness has been diminished by one half through these sad affairs. The three children will not be distinguished by their good fortune, and when you yourself die, you will find it hard to escape the tortures of the knife-bristling mountains and the sword-studded trees. Think of it, husband."

"Most excellent wife, if you are suffering such torments, I will hire priests to say mass on your behalf, and worship the Buddhas, so that you may be delivered from purgatory."

When the wife heard this, she danced upon the earth, and cried piteously, saying: "By such words you only add to the torture of my punishment. You do not heed your father's death, and only think of the woes which afflict your wife. What right have I to complain? All my sufferings I have brought upon myself. You must pay an immediate visit home, and seek out a virtuous maiden of excellent disposition and irreproachable deportment, who can distinguish between the honourable and the lowly positions in a household, and will be able to fulfil the duties of a rational human being. Do not spare money, and let your first care be to find a virtuous helpmate. And in association with each other, serve and reverence your parents, and by filial duty expiate the impious acts of bygone years. And thus will your own fault be repaired and my punishment mitigated." Having thus said, she wailed bitterly, and went away.

Sz In was greatly terrified by what he had seen, and perspiration ran down his whole body. During the following day he could find no rest.

On thinking over the whole thing some little time afterwards, however, he came to the conclusion that his mind must have been wandering, and that no genuine ghost had ever appeared to him. But on the following night, the spirit of his wife again presented itself to reproach and curse him. "You do not believe my words," she said. "Although I may have received every kind of favour from you, whilst I am left in Hades I shall still hate you. I shall watch to see the kind of end to which you will come." Again she wailed, and took her departure.

This time Tsai Sz In was thoroughly aroused, and began to lament his former faults. He sent home funds to hire several priests of saintly reputation to say a ten days mass for his father, so as to secure the escape of his soul from purgatory. He then defrayed the expenses involved in the marriage of his younger brother, and afterwards chose out an excellent maiden for himself, married, and took her home, so that they might fulfil together all filial service, honouring his mother as though she were a bhoddisat or a fairy. He bought his mother new clothes, wine, flesh, and fresh fruit, and did everything he could to show his reverence. His own mind, moreover, he now felt to be much more at rest. He also took his younger brother out to the shop to train him for business. He was diligent also in doing works of merit, and printed two thousand tracts on filial piety for gratuitous distribution, so as to atone for his fault.

After he had kept up these devout practices for some years, and was the praise of the whole village, one night his wife again appeared to him in a dream, and said : " From the time you repaired your conduct, and became filial, your new wife also being virtuous, submissive, and serving humbly in all truth, and husband and wife have been united in atoning for past sin by their meritorious conduct, the judge of Hades has taken ten years off my punishment, and has decided that I need not be transmigrated into a quadruped, but may be reborn again as a human being forthwith. Prosperity has again come round to you. Go on doing good without weariness, carefully avoiding old errors." Having thus spoken, she took her departure.

Tsai Sz In constantly repeated this experience to those with whom he came in contact, and many were reformed by his story. He afterwards made a fortune large in amount, and his three children proved a credit to him, which things he regarded as the distinct fruit of his repentance.

CHAPTER VI

MADAM CROSS-GRAIN

IN the reign of the emperor Kang Hi, there lived a Master of Arts whose name was On Wai Shing, of the Shung Hing prefecture, in the Sz Chün province, peaceable in disposition, and with a character free from grave fault. He had two sons, the elder of whom was called Tai Shing, or Great Completeness, and the younger, Ï Shing, or Secondary Completeness. Tai Shing's disposition was filial and friendly, but Ï Shing's was of a contumacious turn. In his fortieth year On Wai Shing was seized with sickness and died, leaving these two sons, who were insured at least against want by their small patrimony of fields and orchards. Tai Shing's mother, whose maiden name was Cham, was of a perverse disposition, and indifferent to what was equitable, accustomed to take her own course, and accounting might right. She was despised by all the neighbouring women, and nicknamed Madam Cross-grain. Her whole get-up may be imagined.

When Tai Shing had attained the age of twenty, Madam Cross-grain arranged his marriage. The maiden name of the bride was Cheung Shān Ū (Coral). In appearance she was beautiful, and of very attractive manners. She waited upon her mother-in-law with gentle words and bated breath; never failing each morning to approach and ask about the welfare of her new relative, offering at the same time cakes and tea. Fastidiously neat in dress, she manifested her reverence by a grave deportment. But, lo! Madam Cross-grain, who had always been indolent and slatternly in her habits, felt ashamed at seeing Coral so neat and presentable, and began to revile her in a loud voice, saying: "It is quite a commonplace duty for the bride to wait on her mother-in-law; do you think it is some festive gaiety? Why need you be so pert and prim and spick and span, giving such heed to voice and carriage, and deporting yourself as elegantly, as though you had come to my place to put your figure on sale? When I was first a bride, I had ten times as good an appearance as you, and never thought that by to-day I should have grown ugly with age some thirty per cent or more."

This reprimand Coral heard silently with bowed head, not daring to speak in reply. On the following morning she again presented tea and cakes, attired now with severe simplicity, and wearing a well-washed blue tunic, but with neither grease on her hair nor paint on her cheeks. Madam Cross-grain grew angry at the first glance, and said: "Because I spoke a word to you yesterday, now you refuse to wear a single flower, to powder your face, or to put on new clothes. You simply want to exasperate me. You think I don't know! You think I don't know!"

Coral again bowed her head without speaking, inwardly reproaching herself for not understanding the etiquette of service. After this, when Madam Cross-grain ran against a stool, Coral was sworn at. When the fowls would not eat their rice, Coral must again be sworn at. Returning home to visit her parents for three days, on her return she was sworn at for ten days. When Great Completeness saw that his mother was not pleased with his bride, he took Coral and beat her, to comply with his mother's wishes. Madam Cross-grain was pacified for the moment, but at length the disease broke out again. Her eccentricity passed all bounds, and she was without kindness or principle.

When the habit of swearing has been contracted, it is just like the vice of opium-smoking; you can scarcely live without indulging. Like intermittent fever, it is sure to come on once in two or three days. Evil spirits are the cause of swearing no less than of fevers.

A Fit of Temper.

One night, because of some trifling matter, this testy old woman stood in the doorway and swore a great volley of curses. Coral brought a bamboo chair, and invited her mother-in-law to be seated. Madam Cross-grain accepted the invitation, sat down, and with back bent, hand pointed to the sky, and feet pawing the earth, swore in a continuous stream without stopping to take breath. Coral boiled a dish of tea and presented it, asking her ladyship to assuage her thirst a little. After Madam Cross-grain had drunk the tea, her throat was mollified, her temper rose, and her voice waxed louder, and she swore away till the third watch of the night, when at length her voice gradually lowered, and her strength fell by degrees, and her breath gave out; for even a dog's voice will fail through excessive barking. Coral then knelt and entreated her, saying: "I have received what you have to teach me, and shall know how to do better in the future. Now please go to bed and rest, lest you should catch a chill from the breeze, and be calling out all night with stomach-ache."

Madam Cross-grain said, "I must swear! I must swear!" and, propping herself up the night through without sleeping, she swore till daylight. Coral was weeping by her side, and the neighbours came in to exhort the fury to desist. Having lit a lamp, Coral led her to her room to rest, spreading out the bed-quilts, arranging the mosquito net, putting the pillow straight, and then withdrew, wishing her mother-in-law a quiet sleep.

The first thing in the morning, Coral went to enquire after Madam Cross-grain, and saw at once that she could not speak. Her eyes were open, but without light or movement, her hair dishevelled and twisted about her head, and the whole appearance as of one already dead. Coral almost fainted away with fright, but at last ran to inform the old women of the neighhood, who came in a group to see how matters stood. The women chuckled loudly, and said to Coral: "You needn't fear; she only stretched her mouth too wide last night, and, having spent her breath, inflated herself with cold air, with the result that the circulation was checked. Her vital energy is exhausted, but with two or three days' quiet nursing she will soon be hale again."

When Coral understood the reason, she at once brought medicated ginger, and green cassia tea, and spirits of peppermint, to drive away the bad effects of the cold wind. She also purchased medicines to strengthen the constitution, and after several doses the patient could just begin to speak a little, and take her rice. But Madam Cross-grain insisted that some flesh should be brought to make soup which would lubricate her system, and Coral complied with her wishes, and offered it.

It chanced there was much cold and phlegm in the system, and its channels were not yet completely open, and after eating a few mouthfuls of pork, the fat pressed upon her throat, and made her so that she was unable to speak for ten days. At that juncture a doctor was summoned, and when he came he turned out to be a beginner, who did not understand his science. Thinking that inflammation was spreading internally, he gave a decoction of yellow nitre boiled very thick. After Madam Cross-grain had partaken thereof, and it had duly wrought, her eyes sank in her head, and she was so exhausted in all her limbs that she could not sit up, her face becoming yellow, and her bones poking out, so that she scarcely looked like a human being. Her vitality, moreover, became so depressed, and her stomach so weak, that food and drink lost their taste, and she dried away more and more each day. The doctor was skilful in healing chronic virulence, although a prentice hand in other branches of his profession.

Afterwards her son called in a physician who was fairly efficient, so that after a time she could begin to speak again, though with difficulty. And so things went on for some months, and there was to all appearance calm after storm. Coral was secretly delighted, thinking that as her mother-in-law was gaining flesh a little, she would now be able to sleep without anxiety. But, lo! as her voice became a little stronger, she began to curse and to swear, because Tai Shing had left home to study. And inasmuch as the old sickness was pressing on her, she swore at Coral, saying that she had bewitched her husband with fine dressing, and impaired his original disposition, threatening withal that she should pay for it with her life if Tai Shing should chance to die. She also swore at her son himself, because he was a worthless fellow, unable to distinguish between good and evil. Taking little heed of himself, he was demented by doting on his wife.

A Heartless Divorce.

Tai Shing knew that Coral was really virtuous and filial, but there was no help for it as she did not meet his mother's tastes; he wrote a deed of divorcement, and said to Coral: "I have heard that the reason for a man's taking a wife is that she should serve his mother. Why do I then still wish to keep you on as wife? I give you a bill of separation. You are now free to seek some new nest, and to marry another husband. There is no need for you to continue any longer an inmate of my house." Having so said, he turned round, walked out of the door and went away. When Coral heard this, her heart left her, and, taking the document, she tore it into fragments and put them in the fireplace, and then went to her room and wept all night in the darkness. She knew that the past could not be undone, and all that was left for her was to pack up her bundle. So she chose out two or three articles of necessary clothing, but had no heart to think of the list of things she had brought with her as a bride. After rendering a farewell obeisance before the tablets and shrines, she came to her mother-in-law, desiring to speak, but could not frame her voice. With runlets of tears on her two cheeks, drooped head, and downcast spirit, she went slowly on step by step till she had got outside the door, where she paused a moment. Here she recalled how on the wedding day her father, brothers, and uncles, in ceremonial hats and long tunics, had followed her with lighted lanterns till she alighted from the bridal chair, earnestly exhorting her to be dutiful and affectionate towards her mother-in-law. But now, alas! she was driven forth for her unfilial conduct. Cast out on such grounds, how could she return home and face father, brothers, and uncles again! The best thing was to die. When she had thus thought, she drew a pair of scissors from her sleeve, placed them towards her throat, and began to cut with all her might. At that juncture happily a woman came up alongside, who, observing her fierce and excited demeanour, made a strong effort to seize her hand, and, thrusting it aside, said at the top of her voice, "Why are you so furious?" The scissor blades had already gripped her throat, and cut the skin, so that blood was flowing in a stream.

The woman stanched it at once, and, taking the cloth Coral wore bound about her head, hastily bandaged the gash, crying out at the same time, "Save life! Save life!" All the neighbours then came running wildly, bringing pills and powders for wounds and abrasions, which, having been duly applied, arrested the flow of blood. Coral rested herself before the door, her face the colour of the earth. All who saw pitied her, some of them sighing aloud at the sight. Madam Cross-grain only cursed, saying: "You are making a pretence of killing yourself for the sake of involving me. If you want to die, go home to do it. Don't gather a crowd of people before my door to disturb me."

There was a widow in the same clan as Coral, whose maiden name was Wong, who had already heard of the excellent disposition of this disconsolate creature. She knew that Coral had been expelled by her mother-in-law, and, seeing that she was unable to walk because of weakness caused through loss of blood, she led her to her own house and bought medicines to heal her. In less than ten days the mark of her wound had disappeared. After a time Madam Cross-grain came again, and swore, saying, "You low, mean creature, discarded by your husband! why don't you go back to your own parents rather than stay here to be a beam in my eye, and a burning fire in my heart?" The widow whose maiden name was Wong exclaimed: "Eheu! Eheu! what a perfectly ridiculous Madam Cross-grain you are! Your son has already given her a deed of divorce, and put her in the position of a common wayfarer. Is she still your daughter-in-law, that you presume to come and swear at her? Is not such conduct simply beneath contempt? Coral is a distant relative of mine, and if my relative comes to visit me, you, forsooth, must not allow her to stay!" And she in her turn swore at Madam Cross-grain till that venerable person was dumbfounded, and could only swallow her shame and go straight home in dudgeon.

Coral then said to her hostess: " I cannot make this my permanent resting-place. I must now be taking my departure." Packing up her bundle, she went away to live with a great-aunt on her mother's side who had married a man named Lok. She was cousin to Madam Cross-grain, and related therefore to Tai Shing. Advanced in years, and a widow herself, she had a daughter-in-law also a widow, and a little grandson. They lived some distance from Tai Shing, but had been to visit Coral, and had seen how filial and affectionate she always was. Coral accordingly entered their house, and told them some little of what had taken place.

" I know something," said the old aunt, "of my relative's awkward disposition, and how inconsiderate she is. That was the reason why I was rather remiss in going to visit her. It is very cruel that you should have received all this oppression and ill-treatment from her."

" It is not after all on account of my mother-in-law,

That I did not understand the art of being filial and conciliatory was my own fault, and I was therefore fated to provoke her at every turn. I know my sin, and ought to die for it."

"You must not speak thus," said the old aunt. "I know you are concealing things."

A Visit from Coral's Mother.

After the lapse of some days Coral's mother came to visit her, and said: "I was away from home at the time, and did not know at once what had taken place, but have since heard our son-in-law has given you a bill of divorce. Why did you not come back home, rather than find your way here, to moil and disquiet your great-aunt? What reason could you have for taking this course?"

Coral replied: "Your daughter could not shame to face her father, brothers, and uncles again. I am resolved to stay here, and spin and embroider for a sip of coarse tea and a mouthful of rice, and here I will finish my days."

"Who could have foreseen the depths of your miscalculation, my daughter? With all your fine qualities and charms, you need not give way to despair. I shall find a new husband for you with plenty of money and an easy disposition, and with no mother to worry and oppress you, and I shall again give you in marriage."

"I have heard," replied Coral, "that a faithful

statesman does not serve two sovereigns, nor a faithful wife marry two husbands. Whilst I still have a mother-in-law I am unable to minister to, how could I have the effrontery to go into another family? If you insist that I must marry someone else, I shall leap into the river, hang myself, or take poison, and there will be an end of it. I have no wish to live a stolen life in the world of men.

> When blow spring's wet breezes, and the bulb's growth is small,
> And the pools are all pitted with the rain-drops' thick fall,
> On the ooze of the pond-floor the lotos roots seize,
> Unlike the limp willow blooms, adrift with the breeze."

Before she had finished the sentence, there came a choking sensation in her throat, and she fell on the ground sobbing, but unable to give articulate expression to her agitation.

Her hostess, seeing the tear-drops in her eyes, said: "Do not force her too much. Let her have her own way a little. If you press her unduly, she may cast away her own life in a spasm of perplexity, and how would you feel then?"

The mother, wiping her eyes, answered: "I cannot understand how it is that heaven has made you such an incarnate little demon. You may have happiness, and yet you push it aside. You may be a respectable and well-placed person, and you decline the prospect. Your heart is still set upon that miserable old mother-in-law, and you reproach yourself for not having served her with a devotion sufficiently perfect.

You think she humbled and tortured you too little, forsooth! She did not restrain you with enough force, indeed! When I think of the demented old witch, I would like to bite out a couple of mouthfuls of her flesh; and yet you cannot bring yourself to part with her! Your tastes must surely be somewhat mean. Your mother will take the responsibility of finding you a new position, where you will have food and clothing at will; and you will not go, and have set your heart on living a life of starvation. Is not that a sign of unconquerable vulgarity? When you are dying of hunger or cold, do not blame your mother with your last breath. If you will not hear me, I will mutilate myself as the sign of an oath that I have cast you off, and no longer regard you as one of my own children. Then you need not be afraid I shall come to look after you again."

Coral cried incessantly, her mother cried and stormed, whilst the hostess chattered volubly, desiring to play the part of mediator. When her mother saw that it was impossible to change her purpose, she paced to and fro and shook her limbs, and prepared to depart, never even answering the invitation that was given to stay and eat rice. When she had reached the door, she turned her head about, and, pointing with her finger to Coral, said: "After this I shall not recognise you as my daughter, and you need no longer address me as your mother." Thus speaking, she went off in a rage.

When the mother had taken her departure, Coral

remained with the aged relative, to quietly carry out her resolve.

NEW WIFE SOUGHT FOR TAI SHING.

Soon after the flight of Coral, Madam Cross-grain called together the go-betweens, and said: " I have a good son, and should not be sorry to find a wife for him. Now, you matchmaking women, set your wits to work, and find up a taking girl as soon as possible, and send in her horoscope, and when the terms of marriage are settled, I shall fee you handsomely. Other people give two hundred copper cash, or thereabouts, to their go-betweens, but I am going to be spendthrift and pay in silver dollars."

As soon as the go-betweens had received their orders, they each went their way and enquired on all sides ; but Madam Cross-grain's reputation was pretty well bruited abroad ; and far and near parents who had seen the issue of the first betrothment were rather shy of dealings with the family. Who would be willing to let his daughter marry the son of such a harridan ? And thus it came to pass that for two years not a solitary horoscope of maiden was brought back to see if its conditions would dovetail into that of Tai Shing. Madam Cross-grain then sighed, saying : " Most extraordinary ! Can it be that my house is not a good building to live in, and that my rice is not a good grain to eat ? How is it that I can hear of no family willing to intermarry with mine ? Hard indeed is it to find any explanation of the fact."

Marriage of I Shing

Now because I Shing had already reached his majority, it was necessary that steps should be taken to consummate his marriage. The patronymic of the new daughter-in-law was Chau, and her name Tsong Ku, or Paragon Aunt. As soon as the bride reached her future home, Madam Cross-grain began to instruct her that she must be filial and docile, and that with bended head and bated breath she must minister to her mother-in-law. Above all, she must not imitate the evil disposition of the first daughter-in-law (a direction which she carried out to the letter). " Better than she was you must certainly be. In a word, if you are good, I shall be good. Why should not a mother-in-law be fond of her daughter-in-law? The only difficulty that can arise is when the daughter-in-law is not clear about her duty, and the mother-in-law gets a little provoked. If you are only willing to obey, my heart will get into my heels, and make me dance for joy."

But who would have thought it? The wife of Secondary Completeness, in spite of her high-sounding name, Paragon Aunt, was nicknamed "The Heaven-Usurping-Get-Up," and also "The-Gutter-Poultry's-Imperial-Chancellor." If her mother-in-law gave expression in one sentence to a little displeasure, she would stick out her lips and reply with a dozen sentences or more. Every morning she slept till the sun was more than thirty feet above the horizon, and after she had risen, she would set her mother-in-law to wash the plates and bowls, and to cook vegetables and boil the rice; when her mother-in-law would not do it, she swore at her in ringing tones. "Several tens of years old, and cannot do a little simple, light housework. You won't boil a small meal of rice for us to eat a mouthful even! You think you can live with us young folk, and smooth your hair at your leisure, and powder away at your cheeks, and stick in your flowers, and you must moreover keep binding your feet round turn after turn till now." In boiling rice Madam Cross-grain would now put in too much and now too little water, and at one time the rice was too soft, and at another too hard. The Paragon Aunt would then mutter under her breath, and curse in a whisper, as though she were invoking the gods. And she now called her mother-in-law an old tortoise-wife, and now an old dog.

When Madam Cross-grain heard it, she would wax angry and say, "Have you come here to curse me, indeed?" and the Paragon Aunt would protrude her eyeballs and shout: "If I do curse, what shall you do next? I have no fear of your temper. If you like, you can fight it out with me before you sit down to rice." And with the word she would roll up the sleeves of her tunic, and tighten her headgear, and spread out her body, and make a display of strength very much like a fierce tiger stalking down the mountain side in anticipation of a good meal of human flesh.

Now Paragon Aunt was by birth tall, stout, large-boned, muscular, and fierce and savage in temper withal. When Madam Cross-grain saw the fury rushing into her face, as she had been afraid of her thirty per cent. to start with, now that this daughter-in-law was making a practical display of her majesty, Madam Cross-grain rushed out of the door, calling for help and crying for life as noisily as a whole market-place full of people, and jumping about like a live shrimp, and exclaiming, moreover: "I do not know why these dogs of broken-down families should have been brought together to hold me at bay. My whole life long I have been a good and honourable woman, as all my neighbours can testify; how is it that you young people should be so intolerable? Is there any such doctrine as this? Is it not hard indeed that a daughter-in-law should be more ferocious than her mother-in-law?" But Paragon Aunt took no heed to what was said, and the neighbours hid their mouths with their hands and laughed.

That night mother-in-law and daughter-in-law stood at the open door and had a pitched battle of words. Madam Cross-grain cursed till the third watch, and then left off work. But Paragon Aunt cursed on till the fourth watch without shutting up her mouth. Madam Cross-grain now knew that she was outmatched, and gulped down her indignation.

CONNUBIAL ASSIMILATION.

One day the old harridan began swearing at her second son, Ī Shing, saying: "What an old bone of a beggar, what a head of a blind grub are you, to play the part of a son in this fashion! You must surely see your wife is a presuming vixen, always cursing and swearing, and you are her husband, and do not shout a single syllable at her, or give her one passing taste of the stick. What does it all mean?"

Ī Shing replied: "She is rude to me as well as to you. What could come of beating her?"

"According to your view, Ī Shing, she need be subjected to no restraint whatever, and may be licensed to ill-treat her mother at will."

"You are a bit too snappish with me, and always were. Formerly you said of my brother's bride that she was no good. And now you say my bride will not do. Who upon earth will suit you? My wife says of herself that she is very good, and as for me, my verdict is that she will pass muster."

When Madam Cross-grain saw that I Shing was in this mood, she grew still more angry, till at last it brought on sickness. But in her affliction only Tai Shing would call in the doctor and prepare her medicine and tea. Ī Shing and his wife neither knew the general character nor the particular details of her illness, but simply ignored the matter.

Tai Shing then said to Ī Shing: "Brother, you

know how it is our mother is prostrate on her bed with sickness. It comes from the irritation caused by the unseemly conduct of yourself and your wife. You seem not only to be incapable of changing the disposition of your wife by exhortation, but you yourself have degenerated into an unworthy son. Your wife comes of people with a different patronymic. It was through your mother you received your birth into the world. You never reflect how, when you were little, if you were sick your mother would sit all night with lighted lamp nursing you in her lap and ministering to your needs without ceasing, and how, with tears scarcely dry at dawn, unkempt hair, and unwashed face, she would put you on her back and go off to the doctors and get medicine to administer, and pray the spirits and entreat the Buddhas for your recovery, beating her forehead into a wounded pulp with her many prostrations. When you had sickness, your mother was stirred to her inmost soul. Now your mother is sick, and you pay no heed to it whatever. Hereafter you hope to have children and grandchildren. What blessing and honour is there pertaining to parenthood if the offspring is to act as you act? Now, brother, you must attend to what I say. Tomorrow just present yourself at your mother's bedside and enquire after her progress. Ask if you should call in another doctor, if she will eat rice or congee, or if there is any dainty she can fancy. Ask this with a soft voice and bated breath, so that you may comfort your mother's heart a little. That will be more like fulfilling the duty of a filial son. Now can you remember all I have said?"

I Shing, who had borne this just about as long as he could, answered: "Do you think I am stupid? You fear I cannot remember?" And having said thus, he went away.

The next morning, very early, he was in the act of getting up, and Paragon Aunt stormed at him, saying: "Are you mad? It is scarcely daylight, and you are getting up, and rolling the clothes aside and chilling my shoulders. Where are you going?"

"I am going to my mother's room to enquire after her health."

"Do not adduce this pretence of false piety to trifle with me. I know you pretty well, and am sure you are not one of that sort. Who directed you to do this?"

"My brother bade me," replied I Shing.

"You ought to use your own judgment in giving ear to other people; and see if they are worth listening to. You will listen to your brother, and your brother is an idiot; for if he had had any wit about him, he would not have been wifeless now. Probably you intend to discard your wife and follow in the steps of your elder brother? You deserve a downfall if you take pattern by him. In the end you will certainly rue your mistake. Now listen to me, and you may have a happy career. I shall not permit you to go; and if you dare to go, I will bolt the door very early to-night, and not allow you to return to sleep."

"If you wish me not to go, I do not know that there is any very great difficulty in complying with your request. I will come back to bed and lie down again."

Paragon Aunt then laughed. "Now you are a good husband."

When a slow-hearted son and an evil-tongued wife recline on the same couch, they may be compared to a snake and a rat sleeping together.

Tai Shing had expected that his brother would certainly go and ask after his mother's health, but he had hoped in vain; so now he thinks within himself that, as his mother's sickness sprang from care and annoyance, he ought to arrange and have someone always with her to divert her attention and dissipate her vapours by constant conversation. After he had knit his brows and mused for a time, he suddenly brightened up and exclaimed: "I have hit upon the right plan. There is a female relative who is well advanced in years, and has plenty of time upon her hands. Why should I not invite her to come and be a companion to my mother, for the gossip of an old crony may unlock her heart."

When he had come to this conclusion, there was, as it happened, someone going to Mrs. Lok's neighbourhood, and he availed himself of the opportunity to send a message, and the invitation was accepted. From the arrival of the old dame, Madam

Cross-grain's forlornness began to relax a little. In the still watches of the night, when tea was wanted, water was always ready, and the views and feelings of the old ladies jumped together, and not a little conversation went on to beguile the time.

The daughter-in-law of this companion always sent her cooked food from home every day. At one time it would be pork boiled with cuttle-fish, at another fresh fish, soup, or oranges large or small, or sugar cane, or candied fruits. The old companion did not eat much, but Madam Cross-grain tasted and swallowed everything with the utmost recklessness, and satisfied all her fancies. At last, having broken out into a snatch of a song in her merriment, she said: "Well, old crony, fortune has been kind to you. Only think how blessed you are in having such a filial-tempered daughter-in-law. Why, when you have come to see a relative, she follows you with constant presents. Who can say what stacks of viands you must have to eat when you are at home?"

The old companion replied: "The woman who knows how to show herself a good mother-in-law naturally has a good daughter-in-law. We must take things as they come in this world, as you and I both know. For even a little to eat we must be thankful."

"I have no such good daughter-in-law," sighed Madam Cross-grain. "Look at mine, got up as if she owned the firmament and all it contains. I would not even expect mine to buy presents of food for me, but should be satisfied if she were a little less passionate. My only desire is that she will not provoke me so much."

"But when Coral was with you, she was good-natured. If you swore at her, she only dropped her head; and if you beat her, she had no grievance to complain of. The fact of it is, you were rather awkward-tempered in your treatment of her, and, to put it gently, did not err on the side of indulgence."

Madam Cross-grain then groaned aloud and said: "I now see from contrast with the vices of my second daughter-in-law that my first daughter-in-law was really very good. I indeed repent, but it is hard to retrace one's steps. I do not know whether she may be married again, and where she may be gone by this. It is difficult for the north of the earth and the south of the heaven to cross each other's path again. When my ailment is better, I will go and have a peep at your daughter-in-law, and that will do."

MADAM CROSS-GRAIN VISITS HER FRIEND.

After about twenty days, when the sickness was overpast and the old relative had gone back home, Madam Cross-grain came to pay the promised visit, and, as soon as she had entered and quietly seated herself, said: "Now this good daughter-in-law of yours, where is she?"

And the relative answered: "*My* daughter-in-law is not good. It is you who have the good daughter-in-law."

"I do not know where my daughter-in-law may now be — probably married again in some strange place to a new husband. Good or not good, I have no share in her affections and no right to her service."

"Your Coral is still here, weaving cloth at my house for a livelihood. The things sent as presents when I was with you were all bought out of her savings."

Now, when Madam Cross-grain heard this, her heart was stirred, and she gave a long cry: "Pity her, pity her! I cannot understand why she has been so good a daughter-in-law, for she was very badly treated. But if she is in your house, why is she not to be seen?"

Coral then came forth from her room and knelt before her mother-in-law, saying: "Your daughter-in-law has been unfilial, and was unversed in the art of ministering to her mother-in-law. I hope you will be lenient to my sin."

With two hands Madam Cross-grain then helped her up and answered in a fluster: "You are perfectly filial. From antiquity till now you have been unequalled. You top the list. The only thing amiss is that I am old, stupid, and useless, and cannot distinguish between light and heavy in my swearing and railing. Do not blame me. If, after eating rice, you will follow me back home, you will be the blessing of the household."

Coral replied: "If my mother-in-law will only receive back her daughter-in-law and give her a home again, the grace and favour will be like that of heaven itself. I hope you will point out the defects of your daughter-in-law and teach her."

"There will be no need to teach; none whatever," Madam Cross-grain said. "Your old style of filial piety will more than suffice."

The old relative then killed and cut up a fowl and spread a repast, so that they could all feast together in joy. Coral chose out one piece of delicate fowl and offered her mother-in-law, and Madam Cross-grain chose out several tit-bits and pressed them upon Coral. She also begged Coral to drink wine, saying: "It is a good omen for young people to drink wine brought on with the fowl."

When Madam Cross-grain had sipped several tens of cups, her face began to get as red as the rising sun and her neck so relaxed that her head was bobbing to all points of the compass. After the repast was over, and her spirits had risen, and she had fanned herself cool again, she led back Coral home, swinging her arms with great vigour on the way. When she reached the entrance to her own alley, quite a number of people stood by the wayside, and Madam Cross-grain addressed them, saying: "My daughter-in-law had not married anyone else, and she said she must come back home to wait upon me. I could not very well bear to give her up, so I brought her back with me. Is it not a good plan?"

"Good beyond all forecast. Good beyond all forecast," they cried with one consent. "She is a daughter-in-law it would be hard to match."

Upon their arrival, husband of course loved wife, and mother-in-law loved daughter-in-law, and the family was happy and harmonious with the breath of spring in their faces.

HIVING OFF.

But what sort of pleasure was it that Coral's return gave to Ī Shing and his wife? Ī Shing grew angry, and said: "My brother declared at first he did not want his wife, and now receives her back with the utmost ostentation. How can he look men in the face if he goes upon this principle? My mother is still more demented. At first she said her first daughter-in-law was not good; now she turns round and makes her out a gem. What does it mean? This thing does not suit my taste. I must have the patrimony divided, and we will keep separate tables."

When Tai Shing heard this, he replied: "Brother, if you wish to divide, we will divide."

"I insist upon a division," said Ī Shing.

So when they had assembled together paternal and maternal uncles and aunts of different degrees, and the old men of the family whose office was to assess, arbitrate and formally witness to the division of the estate, Ī Shing said, "I must have five or six extra acres of the low-lying field, and seven or eight acres extra of the land on the island, and ten extra fruit trees."

The great-uncles then said: "The proper rule for the division of property left behind by a father is for each brother to take one half. But if the eldest son or grandson who is the responsible representative for the family should desire a little more, there would be no unreasonableness in that; however, why should you want a larger portion than your elder brother?"

I Shing answered: "My brother was at school for more than ten years, and has been in to the examinations seven or eight times. When my brother was married, two bands of musicians were engaged for his wedding; but when I was married, there was only one band of six flute-players. I therefore want a little more out of the estate to make things equal."

Tai Shing said: "Brother, I shall not strive with you. Take your first choice, and I will have what is left."

And thus I Shing got the best fields and the best land and the best of everything, and Tai Shing did not even think of making comparisons. The uncles said: "Such an elder brother is not a man to be made light of, but is one of a thousand. For the past seventy years we have been present at divisions of property times without number, and have seen men contend for a foot of land at the top of a field or the corner of an allotment, and the strife reached such a pitch that skulls were crushed and brows cleft open, and enmities sown that led to deadly law-suits. Sometimes they have striven because of some little inequality in the size of vessels and articles of furniture, and have made so much of their petty apportionments that they have grown red in the face and eyes, and have thereafter been accustomed to meet without speaking. But you seem to look very lightly on these things, and are indeed unexampled in your disposition, belonging to quite a superior grade to the rank and file of mortals."

Tai Shing replied: "The rule for the division of parents' property is not inexorable. If he wants a little more, I will think of it as though our parents had left a little more behind them. Had they left two or three more children to share it, I could not have stubbornly insisted upon taking as much as I have now."

The uncles then clapped their hands with delight, and said: "The ten years' education your father gave you was not wasted. You can understand, and practise what you understand."

Now Tai Shing went out as a school-teacher, so as to be able to maintain his mother, and Coral occupied herself with embroidery and cloth-weaving, so that she might be able to minister to her mother within the house, all dwelling together in joy and peace. I Shing and his wife were secretly glad, thinking now that there would be no ties and no restraints, and that they would be able to have everything to their minds. They set up a table of foreign fashion japanned with gold lacquer, and two bamboo chairs in which they could stretch out their backs, and ivory chop-sticks, and plates and bowls of fine china, and teapots and flower-vases and the like, every article of which was fresh and bright. And thus they dwelt at their ease, the wife as gay as a millionaire, and insisting at every meal upon the best of wine.

One morning, when she had got half through her wine, she bade her husband go out quickly and get some toasted pork thoroughly salt in flavour. He had just wrapped it up in a lotos-leaf when he ran against his mother, who said, "What have you got there?"

I Shing answered: "It is not for you to ask. We have separate tables, and you do not superintend our cuisine now. Well, in fact, this is dragon's flesh. No concern of yours."

Madam Cross-grain was greatly provoked. "Blind grub-head," retorted she, "how contemptuous and insolent you are, speaking without deference in your words and insulting your own mother! I won't allow you to eat it."

With the word she stretched out her hand and made a grab which had the effect of breaking open the parcel and scattering the strips of toasted pork upon the ground. At that very moment there were two great dogs by the roadside, who became perfcetly frantic as they made a rush for the viands. I Shing, stooping to gather them up, found himself launched into a contention with the dogs, who in a trice loosed their grip of each other and bit him several times. Their teeth went through a finger and the drops of red blood trickled down upon the few pieces of toasted pork he had recovered, and also stained the earth. At the side of the road there was a string of beggars, who clapped their hands and laughed away in audible guffaws. I Shing went home, cursing under his voice, in a high state of fury.

When Paragon Aunt had enquired the cause, she also was equally angry, though sorry at the misadventure. Both agreed in blaming their mother and censuring her for lack of kindness. At the four divisions of the year and the eight festivals, they never asked their mother to eat a meal of rice, or invited their brother to drink a cup of wine. When the wife's uncle came with presents and compliments, they bought fish and flesh, and did everything that was possible to *fête* him. And when Paragon's own mother came, they filled heaven and earth with their merry-making, killing ducks and fowls without number.

On the thirteenth of the eighth moon, they invited Paragon's mother to come to a birthday, and prepared a great fowl, four pounds five ounces in weight, and stewed it with lily seeds, chestnuts, red dates, bamboo shoots, vegetables, ginger, and all kinds of condiments. After it was stewed, the fragrance floated round into the next house. I Shing had two sons, and Paragon Aunt even would speak in high terms of their promise. Now the first-born was several years old, and as he saw the dish of stewed fowl awaiting his maternal grandmother, he asked his father, "Shall I go and invite the paternal grandmother also to come and eat rice?"

I Shing said: "First ask your mother, and then we may come to a decision."

Paragon Aunt replied: "You must not go. What would you invite her for? She is an old dog of a mother."

Ought not such language to be punishable with death? A dog indeed she would feed, but not this creature.

Afterwards Paragon Aunt told her little boy to go and buy a pot of oil, and gave him his orders, saying: "If your grandmother sees you buying oil, and asks, 'What have you for dinner to-day?' you must say that we are having raw bean curd. You must not let it out that we are indulging in fowl."

When Madam Cross-grain heard this, she was greatly incensed, and said to Coral: "The universe has in it folk of this sort, who have heart and have it to excess. When the outside mother comes, they kill fowls and exercise hospitality, but man and wife never ask their own mother to eat a mouthful. What use is it rearing sons and finding wives for them?"

Coral laughed and answered: "Well, do not suppose every one is after their cut. There are some who are good and there are some who are bad; but the world assuredly could not be carried on if all were to take pattern by them. Suppose you were invited there to a meal, how much could you eat? To-morrow I will go to the market and buy a plump fowl, and make duck sausages and other things, and you can eat your fill."

Madam Cross-grain said: "How do you make that sausage? I am getting past middle life, but have never eaten such dainties as yet."

The next day Coral was as good as her word. Madam Cross-grain ate to the full, with very great gusto, and stroked her paunch and straightened her backbone in a spirit of perfect contentment, and afterwards, when she met anybody, could do nothing but talk about the virtues of Coral. The physical wants of old people ought always to be divined in this fashion.

Domestic Tyranny and its Fruits.

Paragon Aunt in the meantime was becoming more fierce and contumacious than ever, till at last her lack of self-control brought serious consequences. One day, because there was something that did not just suit her, she seized the slave-girl and beat her most unmercifully, and by one careless stroke fractured the skull, and the poor creature bled to death.

The father of the house-slave was greatly enraged, and said: "Because of poverty, I sold my daughter that you might employ her labour, not that you might beat her to death. Do you think, when you buy a slave-girl, it is according to some private code of your own? Possibly my daughter might hereafter have been wife to a rich man. Who can tell? Could you see into her future destiny? And then there would have been no more selling of daughters into servitude for generations. Now you have killed my daughter, and I have sworn an oath that I shall give you no rest, but shall petition the mandarin to put you on your trial."

He was as good as his word, and made a complaint to the chief magistrate, who forthwith sent out police to arrest Paragon Aunt. Placing chains round her neck, they led her away.

The mandarin, having opened the court for the trial, said: "You mean woman of bad disposition, you took human life, accounting it a thing to be sported with. Now what punishment do you think should be awarded you? Be quick and confess."

The Paragon Aunt, then kneeling, made her petition, saying: "Great officer, your discernment is lucid. I, the humble housewife, have hitherto been a lover of virtue and good works. On the first and fifteenth days of the moon, I have always burned incense and worshipped the gods. How can it have come about that I am charged with murder? It is only because this slave-girl was in the habit of stealing rice to eat, and I caught her in the act, and struck her several times with my fist, and unwittingly fractured her skull. She fell to the earth and died. What strength is there in a poor housewife's fist? It was because this slave-girl had some internal complaint, and her time to die had come. The accident has been used against me, but I cannot be fairly charged with her death."

"Your slave-girl stole rice because you did not give her enough to eat, and she could not bear hunger. You had no compassion on her, and went the length of using your fists upon her body. The poor thing had no strength, and no wonder she died under your evil hand. And according to the statute book, what is the penalty for murder?"

"It is murder to kill with knife or the sword. Is it the same thing to only strike with the hand? This humble housewife cannot subscribe to that doctrine."

"I direct that this low, turbulent woman, who tries to darken the question by talk and deception, shall receive a hundred blows on the mouth."

The police then plied their terrors till the gums of Paragon protruded, and blood trickled on all sides, and her two cheeks stood out as large as a pig's head. Paragon kept alternately sobbing and cursing, and pointing with her finger at the mandarin, asserted that he presumed upon the strength of his position to oppress her. This exasperated the mandarin, who called back the police and bade them give her a hundred more with the rattan canes. They beat till blood and flesh mingled with each other, and yet she would not confess. Calling the police, the mandarin said, "Take this wretched woman and put her in a cell, and at the next court day bring her before me to be charged again."

The father of the slave-girl again pressed his petition, and a second time Paragon Aunt was brought out for judgment, trusting as usual in the sharpness of her teeth and the volubility of her argument. The mandarin then bade the police bring out the press boards, and thus they tortured Paragon till tears and fire mixed themselves in her eyes, and her ten fingers were broken. The pain was so intolerable that she rolled upon the ground, and her breath more than once seemed quite gone, and she had to be revived by copious sprinklings of cold water. When she came to herself, she wept and cried aloud, "I confess I beat her to death."

The mandarin then said: "Now, as she has confessed, you can take her back and shut her up in the cell."

When I Shing saw the suffering through which his wife had gone, it was as though a knife had pierced through his heart, and he hurried home, and went round to men of means, attempting to borrow money with which to save his wife. But nobody would make him any advances, and he was compelled to sell his lands and fields, which realised some three hundred taels or a little more. Out of this he gave one hundred to the father of the slave-girl for "tear-stopping dollars." Another hundred he distributed at the mandarin's court for expenses incurred when the warrant was issued sentencing her to imprisonment for two months. At her release, her face was withered away, and her appearance most ghost-like. The skin had contracted, the flesh shrivelled up, and she was yellow and slender as a piece of firewood, quite unlike the bouncing woman of former days. Thus each received the recompense of earlier misdoings,—the husband in property losses because of his former selfishness, and the wife in terrible personal suffering, the providential penalty for ill-treatment of her husband's mother.

After Paragon Aunt had returned home, I Shing bathed her wounds with medicated wine, and administered sundry pills. Every morning he asked after his wife's health, and when she could begin to walk, humbly assisted her to hobble. The neighbours laughed at his stupidity; but I Shing said: "You need not laugh. She is my wife, and I am following heavenly doctrine. Ought I not to love her?" Alas! he could only love his wife, and could not fulfil the chief duty of loving his own mother.

A Dream of Hidden Treasure.

One night, when Tai Shing was sleeping heavily, his father appeared to him in a dream, and with a pleased expression of countenance said: "You are a truly good son, Tai Shing, and to find a wife the equal of yours would need a long search. Your mother was always of a more or less awkward disposition. Could I have lived with her as a husband for half a lifetime and not have found out that? Your wife, however, has been kind and patient with her, for she is an adept in meekness and reverent affection, and may be accounted truly filial and gracious. The filial merit of both yourself and your wife has been reported monthly in the Western Heavens by the God of the Furnace, and thence reported to great Yuk Tai. Yuk Tai is much pleased, and will hereafter enable your two sons to become literary graduates. For the present he gives you a boon of two jars filled with silver."

Tai Shing answered: "The attainment of literary honour by our two sons is a thing for coming years; but as for the two jars filled with silver, where might they be?"

To which the father made reply: "The silver is in the back garden, under the root of the red thorn tree. I, the humble ghost, have come to announce that fact to you. To-morrow you may dig and take up the treasure."

When the father had thus spoken, with an expression of great benignity upon his face, he passed out of sight.

As soon as Tai Shing came to himself, he aroused his wife, and told her of the matter made known to him by his father.

Coral said: "Are we two then so extraordinarily filial? To speak plainly, if the sons born to us come up to your mark, and if, when we take them wives, the wives come up to my mark, for my own part, I shall be content."

"Well, we must take things as they fall out," replied Tai Shing; "and our first work is to follow the directions heaven has given us."

"If we really find money when we dig, we must first buy a litter of pigs to fatten, and afterwards we must buy several oxen and give them in charge of someone to keep, and every year we shall get a little rice as the price of their hire. When your brother sold his lands and fields too, it was at a very low price; it would be a good thing to buy the property back again. With the remainder of the money we might open a pawn shop, or start a sugar factory, or buy rank and build a library and a large house. Now would not that be capital?"

Tai Shing laughed. "Do you want to be a rich woman all at once?"

And Coral replied: "Well, it is not an uncommon wish after all."

After they had heated water and washed their faces, Tai Shing said to his wife: "Just go into the back street to uncle A Mi's and borrow a wrought-iron spade, and then turn into the next alley to grandfather A Tak's and ask the loan of a second spade."

Tai Shing then took off his gold-broidered cap, his shoes decorated with silk butterflies, his white stockings and long tunic, and, rolling up his trousers and turning up the sleeves of his inner garment, he seized hold of one of the spades, Coral herself taking the other. At first they were full of high spirits and physical strength, and quite taken up with the novelty of the work, and both delved with a will till they touched the roots of the tree. But Coral was accustomed to weaving and needlework only, and after thirty or forty turns began to complain that her arms were feeling weak. Tai Shing laughed and said: "Well, if you have no strength, you can rest a little. Sit down for a few minutes, and after getting your breath, you can dig again."

Tai Shing himself was a man more used to the fan and the pencil than manual toil, a genteel scholar, and how could he be expected to have much physical strength? Lo! after he had dug seventy or eighty spadefuls, he found himself out of breath, and must stretch his back, forsooth! He also complained of pains in his arms, and said to Coral, "You get up and dig a little, for it is my turn to rest now."

Coral laughed and replied: "Well, you need not boast. You of course intend to exchange literary for military pursuits and learn archery." At which Tai Shing laughed loudly.

After they had been digging half the morning, he said to Coral: "Now go home and boil rice, and buy a little pork shank to make soup, and warm a few ounces of good samshoo, so as to animate our spirits and strengthen our arm-bones. And mince a few ounces of lean pork and fry it with an egg for our mother."

"I will keep in mind your instructions," Coral answered.

As they sat down to rice, Madam Cross-grain said: "You two ought not to undertake all that work of digging at the tree roots. Would it not do if you were to hire someone to grub it up?"

Tai Shing answered: "It won't split up into very much firewood, and would scarcely repay the cost of the labour. We have nothing else in view but to take it up for firewood."

After lunch they again betook themselves to work, and digged till late in the afternoon. They had got under the root, and were making apparent headway. Again they applied themselves, till at last a ringing sound was heard, and the glimmer of something white seemed to burst forth. Pushing aside the earth, they made a careful inspection, and, lo! there lay rows of things, white in colour, round in shape, and large as the mouth of a teacup, and a whole jar packed full of them, and they knew that these were dollars. Husband and wife then capered for joy, chuckling to themselves silently all the while.

Just at that moment I Shing came to survey the situation, and in an excited manner, pointing at his brother, said: "Brother, you have no conscience. The stump of the red thorn tree was left us by our father, and I have a share in it. When you took it upon yourself to dig it up without taking counsel with me, you certainly wished to deceive me. Such proceedings will never do. Never. You must give me my half or I shall go to law with you."

Tai Shing replied: "Do not distress yourself; it shall be equitably divided."

"It is all as plain as the figure one," said I Shing. "We surely need not call a family council to settle the matter. Whilst we keep watch here, you can send my sister-in-law into the ancestral hall to fetch the scales."

Coral went forthwith, and Paragon, having heard of the matter, came rushing in post-haste with several baskets full of chaff and emptied the contents on the floor; it would be impossible to say how much there was, the stuff seemed to fill the whole place. And having brought the baskets, she rushed away to put the stand of the scales level and to see that the scale pans were accurately suspended. I Shing handled the weights and kept a close eye on the indicator. Paragon then shuffled the silver into the scale and thence turned it out into the baskets, each basket being about a hundred-weight. The scaleful which fell to Tai Shing was light by a few ounces, and that of I Shing heavy, because the younger brother managed the scale. After all had been weighed out, each brother carried his portion into his own house.

I Shing clapped his hands and jumped in the air, saying: "After all, the great thing is for a man to have a conscience. Never have I injured anyone all my life long, therefore heaven does not hold back from me its good things. When because of that unpleasant business in the law courts I had to spend some hundreds of dollars, it was not with any great mental delight; but now I have got these several baskets full, it is many times more than I lost. Riches are a great help to courage. Hereafter I will buy several more slave-girls, and if they are beaten to death, what will it matter?"

"Such cases can always be managed with money," Paragon said.

To which I Shing replied: "At that time the wheel of fortune had not turned, and made me into a rich man. To-night we will drink a cup of wine and be merry."

I Shing goes Shopping.

I Shing, having brought out a couple of dollars from his store and walked as far as the market, turned into a candied fruit and dried meat shop, He ordered samshoo and white rice and a roast goose and two pounds of roast meat, and brought out his dollars to be weighed in payment.

The cashier turned upon him and said: "Brother I Shing, these are counterfeit dollars. Why do you try and pass them off at a shop where you are so intimate?"

I Shing answered: "They were dug up from under a tree root. How can they be counterfeit? They were certainly deposited there a very long time ago, and in the course of centuries the colour of the silver has changed. If you are in doubt, why not take an awl and bore to the inside, and then you will find out that I am an honest man."

The cashier bored with the awl and said: "Every bit of it is white brass, and it is of no use whatever. It is not even silver-coated, for then the silver of the outside could be used."

I Shing, seeing there was no way out of this strange incident, asked him to put the things down to his account, but the cashier answered: "Well, that gives us unnecessary trouble. You had better not have the things."

He then took back the rice and emptied it out into the hopper again, and poured the samshoo back into the jar, and hung up the roast goose and pork where they were before. And I Shing, crestfallen, went home, not appreciating the flavour of the thing at all, and said to his wife: "As we enter upon this new turn of life, it is thrown in our faces that the dollars are counterfeit. Is it not mortifying? Boil a fowl, and let us have some samshoo and drink to our better luck."

After they had drunk, he said to his wife: "To-morrow you must be quick and starch a new tunic for me. I must go to the capital of the province to buy things."

Paragon asked, "Why?" and he replied: "At the small market-shops of our rural districts the men who profess to be cashiers have never spent a fortnight even in learning the art of their trade. They say good silver is brass. Is it not absurd? The silver we have dug to-day has changed its colour through age. The silversmiths of the city, however, will, I think, be sure to know it. I will bring home two hundred dollars' worth of goods to open their eyes, so that when I go to them again to make purchases, they will not give themselves out to be so dreadfully clever."

All night long the worthy couple were talking of their plans for buying fields and lands, of building houses and purchasing rank, and of all the things suitable to rich people. They got scarcely any sleep; for when they had finished talking, they laughed, and when they had finished laughing, they talked again, till daylight came before they were aware.

The next morning Paragon went out into the street, and her speech was blustering and her voice high and sounding. You might speak to her three times without getting her to pay heed, for she was altogether absorbed in chattering about their own affairs and the security they now had against the fear of poverty. Some who were not altogether disinterested came rushing to their house to sit and talk, congratulating, flattering and praising them by turns, and saying, "How good-hearted and virtuous in disposition they must be, and heaven had used its eyes and at length given them rank and high estate!" Paragon was of course delighted.

It having been arranged that her husband should go to the city on the third day, a list was prepared of the things he was to purchase. It being the cold season of the year, of course they must have silk bed-quilts, crape mosquito nets, lacquered pillows, finely woven mats, long fur robes, and every kind of wearing apparel. Paragon said: "I must also have gold pins and jade bracelets, pearl clasps and silver buttons, a red petticoat and flowered tunic sleeves, every kind of clothing of the grandest description." And lots of ebony tables and chairs and old vases were to be bought in addition. It took two sheets of paper to write out the complete list.

After going on board the boat, whenever I Shing came across a fellow passenger, he would ask which was the best silk shop in the city, and which was the best establishment for furs and also for matting. He would ask those in the forward cabin, and then repeat his interrogatories to those in the aft cabin, and then he would go and ask those sitting on the roof of the boat. And the people said: "You will find out when you get to the city. Do not brag so much."

I Shing retorted: "Do you think it is inferior articles I am going to buy? The sage himself has said, 'Enquire about everything,' and I am just carrying out the classical precept. Do you despise me for one who does not know propriety?"

Everybody in the boat laughed; but I Shing felt no sense of shame, and only made a display of himself, as if it were something very extraordinary in which he was occupying himself.

When he reached the city, he sought out the largest silk and braid shop with as much assurance as though he were a great wholesale merchant, and his mouth wagged and his finger pointed as he said, "I want this and this," and he looked at them all, sample after sample, to see if it was just what he required. At last I Shing said: "Now, you must let me have these at what is a fair figure, and I shall have other transactions with you hereafter. I shall be a customer not for once in a way only." And the cashier gave a shake to his reckoning-beads, added up the bill, and asked the honoured guest to produce his dollars and put them in the scale to be weighed. I Shing fumbled about in a very large style, and at last brought a bag of dollars out from under his waist-band, about a hundred, or perhaps a few over that number. The cashier, having looked at them, said, as he changed colour: "These are all brass dollars. The man is certainly an impostor." And he called aloud to his fellow shopmen to come and search him. All at once the shop was in an uproar, and no chance of explaining himself was allowed to the poor fellow. They bound him with hempen cords right off, blacked his face with ink, and handed him over to the street watchman, who beat him most mercilessly the round of his ward.

The following day I Shing took boat to return home. Paragon, knowing that her husband had arranged to be back on a fixed day, in the evening of the appointed date engaged four or five porters to go to the landing and carry home the furniture and clothing. As soon as the boat had come to anchor, she saw her husband steadying himself by the boat roof and crawling up out of the cabin with down-bent head and dejected mien. "The men are here," she said. "You can put the things you have purchased into their care to carry home for us."

I Shing nodded his head and waved his hand, saying: "Do not be so impatient. Wait till they have got all the cargo out. If they come again to-morrow morning at daylight, it will be ample time." And so the porters went off to their homes.

Paragon said: "Are the things at the bottom of the boat?"

I Shing replied: "Ay."

When they reached home, his wife said: "I think you are looking a little out of sorts. Possibly when you were in the city, holding high jinks in some of the wine-shops or flower-boats, you ate too much frizzle and roast, and your system has consequently become a little feverish. But of course I do not know positively."

I Shing then pulled up the after part of his tunic, and disclosed his wealed back to his wife's view, saying, "Just look at this."

She, of course, saw that his loins were black and blistered, and in her alarm said: "You have employed some man to scrape you as a counter-irritant. How comes he to have cut you so frightfully as this?"

I Shing exclaimed: "Cut, indeed! May the thread of your life be cut!" He then explained that he had been beaten with the rattan, and to mistake this for surgical scraping and cicatrising was nonsense.

Paragon said: "You are now a rich man; what need had you to go and play thief, and get caught and be beaten?"

"I have not been playing thief," retorted I Shing; "but people said that I was an impostor, and had been using counterfeit dollars in payment for genuine goods. And thus I came in for a gratuitous castigation."

"Are all of the dollars bad, then? Your brother is a miscreant indeed. I hear the dollars he uses are all right, and, strange to say, ours are all counterfeit. It is clear he is taking advantage of your dulness. Go at once and insist on having them changed, and if he is unwilling, you need not be afraid to fight him. He is a schoolmaster, and, I will vouch, is no match for you in strength. And if he is still unsubmissive, I will go and tumble down on the floor of his house and sham dead, and do you fear he won't give in then?"

"Capital! capital!" said I Shing. And again they talked over their plans in bed.

Paragon then hurried off to buy sundry herbs and powders, and, having made them up into doses, rubbed them on his back. I Shing thought: "She is first-rate. Her kindness of heart leaves no room for criticism. What an uncommonly good wife she is!"

Paragon observed: "Neither your brother nor your mother comes to ask a word about you. He forgets that he is the same flesh and blood, and she forgets that you are her offspring. If there were any such lack of mutual kindness in us, we should soon grow tired of each other."

I Shing replied: "Well, least said, soonest mended. Let us keep our own counsel. People who act in such ways are scarcely human."

HAVING CHANGED PORTIONS WITH HIS BROTHER, I SHING AGAIN SHOPS.

Early next morning he got up and went off to his brother's schoolroom, saying: "Brother, you are bereft of all conscience, for you have given counterfeit dollars as my share of the treasure-trove, and kept the genuine for yourself; and I have been arrested, and had my face smudged, and made to pose like a black tortoise, and been cruelly scourged. It is intolerable. I do not want these, I want those; change the dollars, and that will do."

Tai Shing replied: "At the time we shared up the money, you held the scales, and your wife held the baskets and shovelled the silver in and emptied it out again. My wife and I never moved a finger in the transaction. How then could we show any partiality to our own interests?"

"Well, I cannot take any notice of all these trifling details; I want to change portions, and there is an end of it."

"Well, if you want to change, that is a very little matter, and it shall be as you wish."

The younger brother then brought his several baskets of dollars, substituting basket for basket, till all had been changed. That night I Shing was happy beyond expression, and said to his wife: "The look of these dollars is very different from the others. I need not be afraid of getting into disgrace now. The provincial capital is not a lucky locality for me. I will go this time to the great trading mart of Lung Tsai, to buy clothes and other things."

After two days, he again got out his paper to write down the lists of intended purchases, recalling them one by one, and asking Paragon from time to time if that were correct or no. Paragon said: "I too forget. Why do you not copy out again the list you took the other day?"

Her husband replied: "At the time they were tricing me up with hempen ropes, I lost my consciousness even, and do you think I had presence of mind to pick up my list and bring it home again?"

After they had thought and conferred together, however, they managed to make out a fairly full list, corresponding for the most part to the earlier one.

I Shing then said: "There is still one very important item I have not remembered to write. I must buy a jar of wine to strengthen my back, and all the joints of my body."

Paragon chimed in: "A little of it might do me good. When I was in gaol, those execrable police, who have no thought of human life, beat madly, and thumbscrewed without any restraint; and although there are now no open wounds in my flesh, whenever there is cold wind or rain, my bones ache more or less."

"Why did you not tell me earlier? If that is so, we must put on our memorandum five pounds of the sinew of northern deer, twelve ounces of tiger-bone grease, and a branch of the tsam herb, and I must bring these things back to strengthen you."

Paragon was delighted, and said: "Be sure you remember. Buy those things first of all."

I Shing replied, "Do not fear lest my memory should fail."

And so he took passage by one of the regular ferries, and reached the great trading mart of Lung Tsai. Having sought out and entered a great silk-shop, he pointed with his finger to the shelves, and said, "Mr. Foreman, I want this, and I want that"; and when they were lifted down, he chose according to his fancy. Having agreed upon the price, I Shing clutched one parcel of dollars, of about fifty taels in value, and passed them over for the proprietor to examine. That person gave a sudden start and said: "Whoever knew the like of this? Yesterday a man took me in with thirty brass taels he tendered in payment, and now you want to try the trick with fifty." He then called the shop assistants to seize and search him. Upon his person they found a hundred and fifty taels, all counterfeit. And they blackened his face, and bound him with hempen ropes, and delivered him over to the street police.

A posse of street police then led him off to the City Hall, swearing at him in their loudest tones, and saying:

People of your order will only suffer themselves to eat rice; our kith and kin you will not suffer to live. We are the guardians of the streets, and why upon earth need you come to patronise us with your custom?"

I Shing whined and said: "From all this you may infer, honoured brethren, that originally I am nothing but a rustic farmer, perfectly straightforward and trustworthy. My brother is a schoolmaster, who will be surety for me, and settle up the whole business. This money was dug from beneath a tree in our back garden, and has not been surreptitiously cast of brass. Ten thousand times I speak the truth, and am not deceiving you." He then prostrated himself before the street guard, and knocked his forehead on the ground, and begged to be let go.

To his entreaties the police replied: "Your many words are of no avail. Strip off his clothes, and beat him."

As soon as they had taken off his clothes, they saw that his back was all black and blue, and scarred with the rattan beating he had previously received. The police then said: "If you are a law-abiding person, how is it you have been beaten after this fashion? You are certainly an impostor, and there is no room for two opinions on that point."

I Shing had no words with which to reply, but he besought them pitifully not to beat him, for the pain of the former beating had not yet gone. "Do you think I am a mere cowhide?"

The police then said: "If you do not wish to be beaten, we must rope you up."

I Shing had never seen anyone suspended with ropes, and thought this must surely be milder than beating. He said therefore, "Well, I will submit to be bound and hung up."

The police then took him and did him up after the fashion called "trussed pig in the roasting-dish." After they had kept him for half the night, crying out alternately for life and for death, and not able to get his wish gratified in either direction, his shrieks for help rending the skies, and his throat well nigh splitting open, the police unbound him. I Shing then knelt before each of the police, knocked his head on the ground, and confessed his sin.

On the following day he met in the street a man with whom he had some slight acquaintance, and borrowed money to pay his boat-fare home. Paragon knew on what date he would return, and, as on the previous occasion, engaged porters to meet the boat and carry back his purchases. As soon as the boat was moored, she saw this martyr of fate coming out of the cabin leaning on a bamboo staff, with bent waist, bowed head, sickly appearance, and walking very slowly and carefully. The clean new clothes he was wearing when he left home had disappeared, an old undershirt only being left to him, such as might be used for stuffing up holes and crevices. Her heart palpitated as soon as she saw him, and she thought within herself, " It is the same mould of bean curd over again." She waited till I Shing had come ashore, and then asked in a whisper how he had fared. " Not a word," said he, " not a word. Help me away home."

After dismissing the porters, Paragon led off her husband, who had to lean helplessly on her shoulder. As they crept slowly along, he talked to the effect that they were not destined to be rich, and that the fates were against them, and that he only got vexation and disappointment for his plans and toils. " This money I intend giving back to our brother."

Paragon said : " The sooner you return it the better. I am afraid that if our luck gets very much worse, we may all be dying together, and how then ? Ill-fated we are, but must not repine."

That night husband and wife rediscussed the whole question, one moment proposing to give back the money, and the next finding it exceedingly hard to part with. The following morning they lighted candles and incense sticks, and worshipped the idol, and then asked for his guidance through an oracle. At first, when they divined with the flat and round tree roots, the intimations were uncertain ; but when they divined with bamboo strips, all the indications were to the effect that it would be unlucky to keep the money. Should they keep it, certain calamity would follow in its train. So the younger brother made up his mind to return it, and bade his wife take it back forthwith.

Upon entering the house, she said to Tai Shing: "Brother, the money is unlucky; we wish to give it back to you."

When Tai Shing reflected a little, he thought it strange, and unconsciously smiled.

I Shing said: "Brother, you need not laugh at me. In the end you yourself may get beaten."

Strange to say, when Tai Shing spent the dollars, the coins were praised for the fineness of the silver, which far surpassed that of common dollars. Every coin weighed a full ounce and two-tenths, and the silvermiths would give an extra tenth of an ounce in exchange for it. Tai Shing, however, was not avaricious, and paid out his coins at the standard rate. Well says the couplet—

> True heart makes true coin.
> Heaven sheds grace on the filial son.

I Shing could not disguise his astonishment, and said: "What an extraordinary thing! Can it be that our father's grave is a place which is lucky for my brother and not lucky for me? When the feast of the graves comes round, I must take a hoe and scratch my father's last resting-place, and waken him up a bit, and tell him to turn round, and not send his luck-making magnetism out on one side only."

When the elder brother heard this, he thought it was very ludicrous. Seeing that his brother's hands were bound, he could scarcely avoid taking pity on him. He constantly gave him money, but the money had no sooner come into his brother's hand than it invariably changed into the hue of brass. It became necessary for Tai Shing to pay his brother's bills with his own hands, and then the money became good again. I Shing said, "Can it be that my brother's two hands are jewel-mines?" and Tai Shing himself could not explain how this came about.

The older repeatedly urged his younger brother to be more filial towards their mother; but, alas for it! I Shing would not regard it, and continued to treat his mother as though she were an adversary.

FILIAL PIETY PREACHED BY AN APPARITION.

One night I Shing's father appeared to him in a dream, angrily cursing and saying: "What an odious and unfilial fellow you are! That mean, frisky wife of yours is far from good, and her husband has grown quite unworthy of his upbringing How truly you illustrate the proverb that people of different characters do not get up out of the same bed! You and your wife have not behaved well to your mother. Do you think I am not cognisant of it? You treat your wife as if she were a pearl or a precious stone, and you treat your mother as if she were clay or mud. It was your mother who gave you being, and not your wife; your mother who, in the weakness of your infancy, attended to your wants, and not your wife;

your mother who found a bride for you, and not your wife. How is it that you only understand the art of loving your wife, and do not understand the art of loving your mother also? Your unfilial sins have already been announced by the God of the Furnace in heaven, and the record of them has been handed on to Yuk Wong, and Yuk Wong is greatly incensed, and has sent forth an unlucky star, so that you may receive the recompense of your evil in scourgings and ropings-up. And—who could have anticipated it?— you are still without repentance; and if you continue as in the past, you and your descendants will soon be cut off, and in your own two persons you must go and be punished in the Fung To Purgatory, whence there is no transmigration." And when the father had thus spoken, he went away in anger.

I Shing awoke in a fright, perspiring at every pore. He called to his wife, who grew angry, and said, " I was sleeping so soundly—why did you wake me up?"

Her husband then repeated to her the angry and vengeful word which his father had uttered.

Paragon said: " It was a touch of indigestion from which you were suffering. Could a man's real father come running in and talking with his lips, especially when there was a daughter-in-law sleeping at her husband's side? He would certainly observe a little more propriety than that. The fathers-in-law of other women do not generally come into their rooms, and it is very improbable he would come right up to the edge of the pillow to carry on a conversation with you."

"There is, after all, reason in your criticism," replied I Shing. "To-night I drank a little wine and ate some pork and salt turnips. It perhaps does arise from the stomach."

"According to his account, you were not filial. Wherein have we lacked that virtue? Have you beaten your mother? or have I beaten my mother-in-law? At the worst we have simply shown a little temper. Let her speak on this subject. How often has she, who is the older, called me first? How often have I, who am the younger, commenced the quarrel? Am I so ill-bred as that?"

"Yes. Your statements are reasonable. I scarcely thought you had fulfilled your duties so well. You talk as acutely as one of the judges of a Superior Jurisdiction Court."

"When I was before the court some time ago, the mandarin was no match for me in speech. He overbore me with his ferocity and his bands of police. It was not as a fair conclusion to the argument that he had me so shockingly beaten. Your mother has a reputation. How is it that she is afraid of me?"

"I always give in to you, for you are a clever woman," said I Shing.

In the eleventh month of the year in which these events occurred there was an epidemic of smallpox amongst children, and the two sons of this couple, seven and five years of age respectively, died. I

Shing and his wife were very sad, and wept night and day.

The murmuring of I Shing could not be checked, and he kept ever saying: "We two have never injured people at any time in our lives: I do not know why Heaven should be so very wroth against us. We have never impoverished anyone, and I do not know what reason Heaven can have for impoverishing us." And every day he repined against Heaven, and murmured against earth, and cursed ghosts, and cursed the good spirits as well.

An old woman belonging to the same clan, who was of a somewhat crabbed and outspoken disposition, and had no fear of provoking resentments, exhorted him, saying: "You assert that you have never injured anyone, but you have done little else besides injure your mother. You say you have never defrauded anyone, but all along you have been defrauding the one who is nearest. I speak without the slightest fear of your wife. It is lucky that I am not the Ruler of Hell, for if I were, I would take the pair of you and drive you into the last abyss of punishment, and there should never be any rebirth for either of you again."

Having thus delivered her testimony, the old woman shook her sleeve and marched out.

When I Shing heard this speech, it made him very angry at the first, but he afterwards reflected that this speech was in perfect accord with what his father had said. "Are my wife and I really undutiful children, so that the universe cannot tolerate us? Those who are hated by men are first disliked by the spirits, and possibly the idols are punishing me."

As Paragon was reclining on the bed, she began to weep, and I Shing rushed into the room, saying: "You need not weep. When I reflect, we really are at fault. Our brother and sister are perfectly filial, and therefore they become rich and have children born to them. We have lost both of ours. When sin is great, it is difficult to secure a plentiful destiny of blessing. If we do not turn round, our woes will thicken, and we shall not be able to escape the sufferings of the abyss. We had better make a new beginning and go back to filial piety, and possibly through the favour of Heaven our past sins may be forgiven. What say you?"

Paragon answered: "As I was lying last night thinking, and comparing my disposition with my sister-in-law's, I felt that I was vastly beneath her level. My temper is turbulent, and you are not very clear-sighted and have been more or less carried away by your wife. If you know how to repent, I am ready to follow you."

Husband and wife that night relented, and set about making themselves filial. They shelled peanuts forthwith, and at the fourth watch got up to make congee, so that they might offer food to their mother the first thing in the morning. I Shing also bought a packet of meat patties to present, and the man and his wife were both delighted to render this trifling ministry to their mother, and were full of kindly dispositions. When she had taken one bowl of congee, they pressed another upon her, and when she had eaten one cake, they plied her with another, and when she could eat no more, they were quite overpowering in their entreaties that she would still continue to eat.

After they had departed, Madam Cross-grain laughed and said: "Extraordinary! For ten years they have scarcely interchanged a word with me. How is it that they are so zealous in service this morning, like A Pang's dog that changed its nature when it grew up?"

When Paragon got home, she at once boiled water, killed a fowl, and sent her husband to buy pork, and that morning they invited their mother to come and breakfast with them, and husband and wife offered the wine-cup, first one showing the mark of respect and then the other, and the old lady drank away to her heart's content. Then turn and turn about they pressed her to take slices of fowl, till the pile on the old lady's bowl of rice, when she took it up to eat, rose higher than her nose. "I cannot manage all this," she said.

"Eat the fowl and leave the rice," said Paragon. "You do not often come to our place." And they urged their mother till she was both full and drunken, so drunken that it was difficult for her to walk, and they led her to a chamber where she could sleep her excess off a little.

In the meantime, Paragon went to her mother-in-law's room, intending to straighten up her bed and spread out her mat and quilt, and put things in order, and perhaps patch or darn, wash or starch a little; but, lo! everything, from mosquito curtain downwards, was so perfectly clean and in order, that she knew Coral's hand was always at work there. Paragon sighed and said, "My fault is great, and there is no wonder at my sister-in-law having such abundant prosperity."

Every day after that, I Shing and his wife were most attentive to their mother, and also deferential to their brother and his wife. But as Fate had determined, after the lapse of about a month, their mother, who was already old, took a chill, sickened, and died. Tai Shing and his wife carried out the funeral ceremonies in a style required by the principles of filial virtue; but I Shing and Paragon cried aloud, and fell on the ground, and rolled lengthways and rolled sideways, just as gourds might roll, and their eyes were swollen to the size of hens' eggs. The Shing U Hau says—

When the tree yearns for stillness, loud roars the storm's blast;
When the child would be filial, both parents are passed.

Paragon in the course of time had more than twelve children; but none of them lived for very long, some dying at three or five years, some living one or two months, some two or three days, and some dying at birth. She wept till her eyes were dry.

One night she said to her husband: "I could never

have imagined that my destiny would be so evil. I only see them born and do not see them live. I have no desire for children, and yet they come; and when they come, they will not stay with us. What can it all mean?"

I Shing said: "I see it all. They are evil spirits which have become incarnate. Other people are remorseful, and ascribe their trouble to the lack of self-culture in a previous life, but you and I have neglected the primary virtue in this life. When I think of our past undutifulness, I do not know how many more downfalls may be in store for us."

Paragon said, "We have already known our fault and become filial."

To which her husband replied: "But, alas! the time was so short, our beginning was too late. If it had only been earlier by three or five years, perhaps our children would not have died. Or if our mother had lived three years longer, we might have reduced the sum of our sin a little. But, alas! everything was against us, and when we wished to be filial, our mother died. Little heed is it that Heaven pays to human wishes as it makes ready inevitable downfalls."

The man and his wife lamented as they lay on their pillows till the third watch, when I Shing again dreamed, and saw his father approaching him with the message on his lips: "To punish your sin it was just that your children should be taken away. You and your wife deserved after death to taste the pains of hell, but because of your repentance and amended conduct towards your mother-in-law, and the sincere filial service you rendered for the space of two months before her end came, you are still preserved in life. Your destiny originally was to have had five sons and ten grandsons, but that has been changed because of your shortcomings in filial virtue. As for the children beyond this number, they are only unhappy ghosts, who have stealthily glided into the life of the flesh, and have come of set purpose to afflict and anger your wife. The overbearing tyranny of your wife was hard to expiate, and had to be punished in this way."

I Shing then enquired, " Father, have the children I buried escaped hell ? "

And he answered : " They have escaped. Lucky were you in being able to show so much zeal and energy before your mother died. If it had not been so, within the space of a month you would have been reaping your reward amongst the sword-bristling mountains and knife-studded trees of the underworld."

I Shing then said, " Am I to be left without incense and worship after my death ? "

The father answered : " You may beg a child from your brother and adopt him as your successor, but you will leave no legacy of blessing as his heritage. His descendants will be few and unprosperous, unlike your brother's succeeding generations, rich and renowned age after age."

After thus speaking, his father vanished.

I Shing awoke in great fear and told the dream to his wife, who said: "We must take our vexations and disappointments quietly and without murmuring. But when the subject of purgatory was introduced, how was it you only asked about yourself and not about me? All your life long you have been forgetful of others."

Coral bore three sons, two of whom became doctors in literature, and Tai Shing gave over one of his younger children to his brother for adoption as his successor. To the present day the descendants of Tai Shing flourish in a remarkable way, but for three generations I Shing's descendants were only few in number and comparatively poor.

CHAPTER VII

THE NINE DEMON INCARNATIONS

WHY good men should suffer reverses, vicissitudes, and cruel bereavements, is a problem that has perplexed the Chinaman just as sorely as the Arab, the Israelite, and the Englishman. The Chinaman thinks he has found the answer to that question in Buddhism. Sins committed in some previous state of existence are supposed to explain much that would otherwise be inscrutable. If a Chinaman had written the book of Job, he would have added to the three friends of the patriarch a fourth, who would have discussed the problem of Job's life in the light of the oriental doctrine of the transmigration of souls. The following story will incidentally illustrate the place of this theory in Chinese thought, as well as show what a piece of admirable machinery the Chinese Competition Wallah gives to Providence for the reward of virtue.

Mr. Wong Chü Wai was a wealthy gentleman who lived in the province of Chit Kong, the bulk of his property having been inherited from his forefathers.

At the age of eighteen he married a Miss Tsui, who, in the course of the first fourteen years of their married life, presented him with nine sons. Uncommon prosperity was vouchsafed to him, both in the affairs of his business and of his family. For the first half of his life, he never did an act that by any stretch of charity could be accounted meritorious. At the close of that period, however, the district in which he lived was visited with famine, and men died in numbers defying all computation. One day his wife said to him: "We have more than enough money for our domestic requirements, and our children will be amply provided for in the future. The year is one of calamity, and multitudes are dying of want. How can we sit quietly down without making any attempt to save the people, and gaze at these faces so full of grief? I should like to spend a few thousand dollars in purchasing rice for distribution amongst the perishing, but do not know whether you would favour the idea or not."

"What you propose, good wife," replied Mr. Wong, "is most excellent. It is said that when men of olden times did good works, the recompense followed to their descendants. And in this case all that you suggest is, of course, well within the compass of our means. Works of this sort are done on behalf of Heaven."

As the result of this conversation, he put up two booths in which to distribute rice soup, one for men and the other for women. Having first sent off an order for rice to the value of six thousand dollars, he fitted up the booths with all necessary furniture and utensils. His original intention was to provide relief only for the people of his own village, but when the preparations he was making became noised abroad, people unexpectedly began to stream in from every direction. In the course of a fortnight the supply of rice ran out, and the peasants within a radius of forty or fifty miles kept trooping in without intermission, husbands leading wives who were crying out in distress, wizened, hunger-bitten octogenarians, leaning on staves, and infants in arms. The buzz was like that of clouds of summer insects. After a single meal, many of the poor wretches would prostrate themselves in gratitude a hundred times.

Without being at all conscious of the change, Mr. Wong grew into a hero and a philanthropist. Money was spent without the slightest restraint, and quite a little army of helpers enlisted themselves to further the relief work, who carried water or fetched firewood, and darted to and fro upon various errands with the speed of lightning. The gentlemen of the place spread themselves out in rank and file, as though engaged in the distribution of commissariat stores in a military encampment. The work was prosecuted without interruption till after the second decade of the fifth moon, when the crops were ripe, and the people had all gone back to their homes.

The total outlay reached a sum of seventy thousand dollars, an expenditure, however, that never occasioned Mr. Wong one moment of regret. At a time when the stress of extraordinary calamity was felt by the people, he was delighted to have had this opportunity for well-doing.

From this time forth his name became known hundreds of miles away, and when he had occasion to travel, he was pointed out as a god in human form. "His sons will certainly rise to the highest literary distinction," was the popular comment upon his benevolence. Mr. Wong and his wife were, of course, gratified by these complimentary prophecies, and complacently remarked to each other, "Doers of good are sure to be rewarded. The five blessings will alight at our door."

Not very long after Mr. Wong had lavished so much of his fortune in charities, one of his sons was suffocated, and another fell and was mortally injured, and by the end of the second year the last of his nine sons had died. The people mourned with one consent, some exclaiming: "Heaven has sightless eyeballs, for it has brought tribulation on a good man. No wonder the world should have in it people who will never do a pennyworth of charity." Others observed: "Famine comes because it is the decree of Heaven that a certain number of people should perish by hunger. Wong Chü Wai, in saving life through these extensive benefactions, has made it plain that he is contending with Heaven. It is a sin to resist one's parents. How much graver a sin is it to fight against the purpose of Heaven?"

The stricken mother shut herself indoors, and wept day after day, till her eyes were swollen to the size of hens' eggs. She scarcely ever ceased murmuring and saying to herself: "I thought the practice of almsgiving would bring recompense to us, but to my surprise there is no merit in it at all. If I had only known in time that charity was opposed to the will of Heaven, I would not have spent a single cash. Now, not only is a large part of our wealth gone, but all our children have died. Is a life so desolated worth the keeping? The best antidote to all this will be suicide." But had she surrendered herself to these first thoughts and inclinations, and taken refuge in death, the tangled skein would never have been unravelled.

Some of her friends said, "If you could only win a visit from a fairy, you might come to know all the ins and outs of retributory law." Acting upon this suggestion, she lit incense sticks and candles, after first sweeping the court of the house, and began to recite sundry incantations. As she was prostrating herself toward the open sky, an attendant upon the Goddess of Mercy gave some sign of his presence in the air. The instruments of divination were brought out and placed in the hands of a youth quite ignorant of writing. Under his mediumship letters flew into shape clear and unmistakable. The oracle thus dictated said: "It is perfectly natural that Wong

Chü Wai should be grieved and murmur. But are you acquainted with the character of some of your ancestors?"

Mr. Wong bowed, and said, "No."

"Well," replied the oracle, "in his last incarnation but one your father fulfilled all filial and fraternal claims. His unstinted generosity proved the salvation of many. In consideration of that, at his last incarnation he was born to wealth and plenty. But, forgetting all too soon the tradition of his past virtue, he hungered after wealth, and made gain his first concern, and trampled whole families into the dust, till at last the cry of his oppressions reached up to heaven, and the spirits of the firmament were incensed against him. In punishment of his avarice and cruelty, nine demons were sent down to incarnate themselves in the bodies of your children. Whilst your father stored up wealth for his descendants, he at the same time bequeathed them a legacy of resentments, of which these demons were to be instruments. You, of course, were hoping that your nine deceased sons would grow up worthy men and bring honour to the family. Had they lived it would have proved otherwise. They would have turned out gamblers, thieves, adulterers, and would have covered the family name with disgrace. Heaven and earth have been alike moved by the good work your wife planned, which has saved many thousands of lives, and God has therefore called back the nine spirits of evil which had become incarnate in your family. It has been decreed, moreover, that you shall now have five sons, two of whom, together with their sons after them, shall be brilliant scholars, and revive the glory of your house. Away with this grief!" After making this intimation, the apparition vanished.

In the course of the next eight years, the five sons promised by the oracle were born. Upon reaching manhood, they all became literary graduates. By the third of these sons, Mr. Wong Chü Wai had two grandsons, whose careers were very remarkable. Whilst scarcely out of their boyhood, they took their first degrees in arts. During one of the examinations, they fell in with a renowned college don, and attended one of his lectures. The theme of it was the opening paragraph in The Great Learning: "He who in his preferences and antipathies is in agreement with the preferences and antipathies of the majority, is the father and mother of the people." The text was explained with great subtlety. Several hundreds of students were present, but most of them looked upon the homily as trite and dull. The brothers, however, were quite captivated by the exposition.

At the age of twenty or thereabouts these two grandsons took their M.A. degrees with honours, and then went up to the imperial capital for more advanced examinations. The man who had given the lecture to which they had listened with such interest some years before, happened to be Literary

Chancellor, and gave out as a theme for essay-writing the very text on which they had heard him speak. To such good purpose had they listened, that the chief points of the lecture came back to them, and their papers were naturally placed at the head of the list. This gave great dissatisfaction to the other competitors. "If no corrupt influence had been at work, was it likely that two brothers would stand side by side at the top of the list in the same year? And in addition to that, their essays are somewhat uncouth in style, and at variance with the standard commentators."

The Prime Minister, who had been at feud with the Literary Chancellor in the past, and was looking out for an opportunity of indulging his spite, took up the cry, and in a formal memorial called the attention of the Throne to this widespread suspicion. The memorial was received and handed over to the Board of Rites.

The Board of Rites recommended that the examination should be declared null and void, that the Literary Chancellor should be degraded, and that the first of the two brothers should be debarred from competing at the next examination.

When the next examination was about to take place, an old scholar, who had acted as tutor in the Prime Minister's family, asked the Prime Minister to use whatever influence he might have, and get his essay placed first on the list. The Prime Minister replied, "It is true the Emperor and I fix the order of the first three essays, but how can I distinguish yours from the others?" The old scholar then suggested that he should write one column of characters in ink a little fainter than the rest of the paper. The hint was approved.

Upon the day of the examination, the younger brother went into the hall with very little heart for his work. He thought within himself, "What is it to me to be striving after honour when my elder brother has been rusticated, and the Literary Chancellor has been degraded from his office?" The reflection made him dreamy and languid, and very little vigour was it that he put into the work of grinding his stick of Indian ink from time to time on the ink stone where he had to dip his brush for writing. The natural consequence of this half-heartedness was that some of the columns in his thesis were very faint. At the assessment of the essays, this manuscript was one of the first to fall into the hands of the Prime Minister, who at once jumped to the conclusion that it must be the work of the old tutor he had clandestinely arranged to place at the head of the list. He handed it to the Emperor, saying: "This essay is certainly very meritorious. The writer of it should carry the palm of the examination. Will your Imperial Majesty approve?"

The Emperor observed, "The style is good, but I dislike the faintness of some of the handwriting."

"The characters are well-shaped in spite of the

occasional faintness of the ink. If it please your Majesty, let it rank second on the list."

"If, all things considered, it is first in your judgment," said the Emperor, "let it so stand."

The name at the top of the honours list, when it was published, was that of this brother who held the second place in the examination which had been declared null and void because of the unjust suspicions to which it had given rise. When this was pointed out, the Emperor became angry with his Prime Minister, and accused him of stirring up false accusations against the Literary Chancellor which had led to his degradation. "How is it," said his Imperial Majesty, "that you yourself have put this selfsame name the very first on the list?" He then abused the Prime Minister till that august official grew red in the face, and did not know where to hide himself for shame. The Emperor restored to his original rank the degraded Literary Chancellor, and at the next examination allowed the rusticated student to come back to the capital and compete again. The young man who had been under a cloud proved the genuineness of his merit by taking the first place, and ultimately became a member of the Imperial Academy at Pekin. In the course of time the younger brother filled at intervals the highest official positions in the administrations of several of the chief provinces.

CHAPTER VIII

THE TOUR OF A LIVING SOUL THROUGH THE UNDERWORLD

UPON the occasion of a public holiday, Teng Lān Kat, M.A., of the Cheung Chau prefecture of the Fuhkien province, made a pilgrimage to a mountain. He was about twenty-four years of age at the time. Taking with him a jar of wine, he wandered at will on all sides of the mountain to enjoy the various views. Only the fir trees were green, for it was towards the end of the year, and all the other trees had shed their leaves. When he had reached the crest, he sat down and gave himself up to soliloquies, varied with sips of wine. All at once a violent wind arose, and, whisking up the leaves that covered the ground, whirled them round in a tumultuous circle, as though there were something strange present in the air. Lān Kat said, "This is a most singular gust of wind, and must surely betoken the passing of a spirit." Without more ado he poured out three cups of wine as a libation upon the earth, and the wind-tossed leaves made another revolution and then passed out of sight. All in an instant he felt as though he were intoxicated and had fallen asleep, and a man clad in azure raiment seemed to be standing before him and making a bow.

"Mr. Teng," said the apparition, "you are an estimable character, and I am greatly indebted to you for the libation of wine."

Lān Kat then asked, "And who are you, sir? and what did you mean by the remark you just passed?"

The figure in azure raiment then said: "I am not a human being now, but one of the message-runners of the underworld. I have been to take a despatch to the guardian spirit of a neighbouring city temple, and my route lay near by this spot. In my lifetime I was passionately fond of wine, and when I suddenly smelt the fragrance of it, I was unable to restrain myself, and have loitered here for a few minutes. Warmly do I thank you for your kindness, which has so delightfully relieved the thirst for wine in my throat. Inasmuch as a benefit of this kind has been conferred, why should the pouring out of your wine be called a libation?"

Lān Kat then put his hands together and made obeisance, saying: "Since you are a message-runner from Sheol, you will know all about that mysterious region. It is said there are eighteen realms of punishment there, but whether it is so or not I cannot say. Often have I wished to make a tour of investigation, but the subject is obscure, and there is no pathway. It is now my good fortune to meet with you. Could you permit me to accompany you, so that I may see for myself?"

"That is an easier task than bean-picking," said the man in azure, "which compels a man to bend his head."

Teng Lān Kat said, "But if you take me to see these things, you must give a guarantee that you will bring me safely back."

"Certainly," said the ghostly visitant. "Do you suppose I am going to take you to your death?"

The two thereupon set out together and walked side by side. All at once they reached a place where the brightness of the sun was obscured, but in the gloom they could still see great crowds hurrying to and fro. At last they came to a hall, and as they halted before the entrance gates, the azure man said, "Stand here awhile, till I have delivered my despatches to the judge, and I will afterwards accompany you. If through the press of business I should happen to be a little longer than I expect, you need not be anxious."

On each side of the entrance Lān Kat noticed antithetical sentences of ten characters, each graven on iron. "Of all types of wickedness adultery is the foremost." "Of all human virtues filial piety is the crown." As he stood watching, he saw multitudes of men arrive at the portals, some carried in sedan chairs, and some riding on horseback, some squatting in carriages and some in cages, some wearing a framework of wood round the neck and some trembling in every limb, some with downcast faces and with scarcely any breath left in their bodies. And of those who were coming out of the hall, some were so glad they could scarcely contain themselves, some were weeping and crying aloud, some were carrying great burdens, and some were clad in rags and tatters; others were coming forth in cow, horse, dog, and sheep skins—in the likeness, in fact, of everything on the earth and under the earth. And in the far background he could see, as though it were under his very eyes, mountains bristling with knives, and trees spiked with swords, seas of gall and wormwood, and pools of blood.

In about an hour the ghostly despatch-carrier returned, and said, "You have had to wait a long time, but I was delayed."

"Then, after all, Purgatory is no mere myth," replied Teng Lān Kat. "For a long time have I been a student of literature, but always felt doubts on this question."

The man in azure raiment answered: "History shows that within a hundred years, at the least, virtue has always attained its reward, but the joy has had its limitations; and those also practising wickedness have met with disaster, but a term has been appointed to the suffering laid upon them, and such, moreover, is the motive of all the destined vicissitudes of life. Those whose virtue is great, such as the sages and heroes of antiquity, are made to dwell in heaven and receive happiness for thousands of centuries. Is not that reasonable? And those who are very wicked, such as the famous rebels and pirates of history, are made to endure disaster and abide in the gloomy underworld for equally long terms of years. Answer to yourself, Is not that perfectly equitable? And as to the virtuous or the vicious mediocrities, there must needs be one to pronounce upon their doings and adjust their destinies, so that each may receive a fitting recompense. Never say that the things which the eye cannot see are necessarily fictitious. The dragons and phœnixes, together with the famous kings and lawgivers spoken of in the ancient classics, must be fabulous if we once lay down the rule that what the eye sees is true, and what it does not see is false."

"But there is book-proof of the matters you have just mentioned."

To which the man robed in azure replied: "But it is not only for the marvellous things of antiquity that we can adduce the evidence of books; is there no such evidence in favour of Purgatory and its penal disciplines?"

"What you affirm is perfectly right, and it would be difficult to refute your argument. But how is it that you, who are evidently a literary man, have to fill this post in Purgatory?"

The dweller in Purgatory replied: "In my early life I was a scholar, and devoted to the pen. This was my only offence, that I did not believe in rewards and punishments after death, and when people conversed of such things, I always laughed a trifle scornfully, and so weakened the foundations of virtue in some men. Embarrassment and failure attended me in life as the penalty of my mistake, and at death I was compelled to fill this post of spirit-courier, and race here, there, and everywhere. Various circumstances tended to draw me towards you, Mr. Teng, and I have assumed a form so as to have the opportunity for a little chat with you. That you are such a sympathetic listener has led me almost unconsciously to pour out my inmost thoughts, and you will be able to help me to atone for my former offences by making these facts known."

Teng Lān Kat said: "Not a little of my stupidity disappears as I listen to your conversation. I will now trouble you to take me through these eighteen regions of torment."

The azure man then led him to a place so dark and damp that the terror of it was enough to make one's hair stand on end. The guard at the entrance shouted to Teng Lān Kat, "What is your business?"

"He is one of my particular friends," the ghostly guide interposed, "and I have brought him here for a little round of sight-seeing."

The sentinel then said, "If he is one of your acquaintances, brother, he may go in at will."

First Region of Torment.

Upon entering the first department, he saw ox-headed and horse-faced tormentors taking guilty souls and beating them as they were hung up with hempen cords. In their hands these fearful beings grasped little bundles of iron rods of the thickness of the stem of a bamboo tobacco-pipe, and four or five feet long; and having beaten their victims from head to foot, they untied them and took them down again. And then hanging up other guilty souls, they beat them after the same fashion, and the souls wailed without ceasing, saying, "We are afraid. Do not beat so much. We hope you will do it with a lighter hand." To all which the ox-headed lictors replied, saying, "You were accustomed to beat others severely, and now it is our turn to beat just a little. You could not very well be ignorant of the fact that those whom you were in the habit of beating used to suffer."

The majority of the condemned souls they were beating were cruel women who had ill-treated their slave girls and dependents. There were also the souls of greedy and tyrannical police, who had forcibly taken men's substance, masters who had oppressed their apprentices, craftsmen who had ill-used their pupils, blaming them unjustly, and wanting in all human tenderness, had given rein to cruel and domineering tempers. Wrong repays itself by wrong, and history is a series of retributive cycles.

All at once a prisoner was brought in with an official button on his hat, fine shoes to match, a necklace, and embroidered robes, who displayed a bold and lofty manner without any trace of fear. As the tormentors proceeded to strip off his clothes and remove his hat and shoes, the prisoner gave a mighty kick, at which they started for a moment in surprise, and said, "What's the matter? Are you insane?"

To which the proud prisoner replied: "It is you who are really insane, for in your audacity you seem to have lost all power of discriminating persons. You are stripping me as though you were highwaymen."

The gaolers thereupon hid their faces and laughed.

"What kind of person do you assume me to be by this treatment?" said the ex-mandarin. "In past days I have filled the position of district magistrate, and have had a hundred villages under my jurisdiction. A high official though I am by position, you treat me as though I were a common thief."

The ghostly gaolers replied, "Although you were a mandarin, you ought to have been called a felon."

"Of what crime have I been guilty?" asked the braggart victim.

One of the gaolers answered, "When you were just now before the tribunal of the spirit world, it was said you had despoiled the people more cruelly than if you had been a robber, and you affect ignorance of your offence." The other tormentor turned to his companion and said, "Do not throw away all these words on him, for I hate this waste of breath. The judge bade us beat him eight hundred blows; let us administer the prescribed number without any more palaver. When we get hold of bad mandarins, we must lay on a little more heavily than for average victims. Grip him and trice him up." As fate would have it, this mandarin was fat and white-skinned, a man of much flesh and little bone. After the staff had been laid upon him a few times, he screamed out in agony, till his cries must have reached the very clouds, sobbing out, " I will not claim now that I am a mandarin, but confess that I was a robber." The tormentors all laughed in chorus, and even a poor woman who was hung near by under torture could not help joining in their guffaws.

On all sides of this vast building, at a distance of about five feet from each other, people were hung up to be beaten. When those who were hung up cried out too distressfully, the tormentors began to beat more furiously, as though they were exasperated by the cries. Some received three hundred, some five hundred, and some a thousand blows. Two hundred was the minimum. Of the victims there were both men and women, young and old. As soon as one group passed out, another came in. An official recorded the number of blows, and, when the sentence had been carried out, presented the report, and dismissed the victims in accordance with the instructions of Yama. Of those tortured, some were afterwards changed into beasts, and some re-born as men, and some still kept in the under-world, so that they might receive further punishment. Where the superior officers sat were a number of inscriptions urging men to beware of evil because of the miseries it must entail after death.

Teng Lān Kat asked, "How is it that there are such multitudes who are here suffering punishment?"

The man in azure raiment replied: "How many inhabitants, think you, are there on the islands of the four seas and throughout the eighteen provinces of the empire? In some places the prevailing customs are bad, and in other places good; and good men are at times to be found in bad districts, and bad men in good districts. How can the mandarins who rule in the realms of the living always distinguish between good and bad? They can simply pick out conspicuous offenders and deal with them. Ask yourself how many bad men are there in one district who have never been brought to justice,—the unfilial, the unbrotherly, the unrighteous, the inhuman, of whom you hear? The sins with which criminal justice amongst men deals are sins of the body and not of the mind only; but the sins avenged in Hades are of both classes: covetousness, impure thoughts, schemes of oppresssion, jealousy, and every kind of vicious disposition. Wherever there is any iniquity of thought, although no outward evidence of it may have appeared, it will not be overlooked by the avenging spirits. A tiger in the far-off mountains that has never crossed the tracks of human life is put down as an evil beast the moment it is seen; although there may be no human flesh in the tiger's jaws, its heart covets a whole human body to tear and devour."

To all this Teng Lān Kat replied, " It is shrewdly spoken."

SECOND REALM OF TORMENT.

After this he was led into the second realm of Purgatory, where he saw hundreds of couches spread out. Many of these couches were planted with thorns, and victims were stretched upon them, some on their backs and some on their faces, pressed down by heavy stones and bound hand and foot so that they could not escape. The whole body was agonised by the process, and the victims were crying out day and night. Of those enduring this punishment, some were in beds alone, and some in couples and in larger companies, without distinction of sex. The beds were of various sizes, and suited to the years and the figures of the victims.

Teng Lān Kat observed : " The punishments I see are of different kinds, because all the sins cannot be put into the same category. Some sins have sprung up in the heart during times of rest and seclusion, and some have been deliberately planned. There are those who, unable to think out their schemes of evil in the bustle and turmoil of the day, concentrate their attention when they close their eyes, and plot things of which nobody has any suspicion. Of the entire sum of cunning schemes, the majority are hatched in bed. Sensuality associates itself with the couch, and must be punished on couches. Undutifulness towards parents and family dissensions often arise from the tittle-tattle indulged in by husbands and wives after they have retired for the night, and must be punished on couches. Those who were parties to secret assignations suffer on the same couch, for companions in unlawful pleasure must share each other's society in punishment. Where wicked aims and tempers were cherished in solitude, the couch is occupied alone. Where more than one transgressed in precisely the same way, whether the culprits be few or many, they are put together on the same couch."

Third Realm of Torment.

After thus speaking, the guide led him into the third realm of Purgatory, upon seeing which, new questions had to be asked and answered.

"Why are some here having their tongues torn out and their lips cut away?"

To which reply was made, "The penalty is one carried out upon those who have been guilty of reckless libels, slanders, and cursings."

"And what about those whose eyeballs are being gouged out, and whose eyes are streaming with blood?"

"These did not recognise the providential gradations of society, and looked with disdainful glances upon their betters."

"Why should some be condemned to have arms hacked off, and fingers sliced away?"

"These stole their neighbours' goods, and in some cases pointed the finger and incriminated the innocent."

"Why do some have their legs slashed in two, and their heels whittled and pared?"

"These were kidnappers, or seduced others into false and corrupt paths."

"Why are some having their breasts amputated and their chests torn open?"

"Their breasts were full of plots, schemes of usurpation and tyranny."

"And how about the victims whose hearts are being plucked out, and who endure disembowelment?"

"These were impostors, and addicted to all kinds of knaveries."

"Some are being hooked up by the back, as though about to be weighed, and the faces of others are being mutilated with knives?"

"These were without backbone in their transactions, and had no care for the skin of their faces" (no sense of self-respect).

"Why is molten metal being poured into the mouths of some? and why is offensive matter being smeared over the bodies of others?"

"These coveted unrighteous riches, and those had no shrinking back from evil reputation."

"A man's pity is stirred as he looks upon sights like these," said Teng Lān Kat.

The man in azure replied, "You think the victims

should be pitied, but Yama thinks they should be abhorred."

Teng Lān Kat then asked, "To what Purgatory do the souls of robbers go; for they are the most noxious of all offenders, and bring upon the community evils that are very difficult to bear?"

To which the guide made answer: "Robbers are of many grades, and cannot all be spoken of under one category. There are both the strong and the weak, the secret and the open, the fierce and the timid. The name is given to them because of their acts, and those acts may be few or many, grave or trivial. Most of the robbers are in the ninth region of Purgatory, where the trees have swords for foliage and the mountains bristle with knives. The rest of the robbers are variously dealt with in the other departments of the underworld. At times the sin a man does in his lifetime may be wiped out by the legal punishment to which the criminal courts on earth have condemned him, or by personal pain and suffering whilst still in the flesh. Now and again the guilt may be expiated by the blight of crops and the loss of fields and orchards, by the untimely death of wife and children, or by the worthlessness of children and grandchildren. In the process of human affairs every conceivable condition may occur to modify the sentence. When an offence has been unexpiated, or there is any degree of uncertainty about the character of the expiation, the economies of Purgatory are brought in to adjust the balance. Sometimes the blessing merited in a previous state of existence may not be due to unfold itself for a while, and there may be trouble in the family and unsettlement in the age without any specific relation to the sins of contemporaries. The causes of sorrow and suffering may sometimes lie outside the range of the passing life."

To this interpretation Mr. Teng Lān Kat answered, " The explanation given is quite exhaustive, and you evidently understand the subject in all its bearings."

FOURTH REALM OF TORMENT.

Coming to the fourth division of Purgatory, they saw wretches put into revolving mills and ground till the earth was sprinkled with their blood, as well as into huge mortars, where they were pounded under pestles worked by the feet, till fragments of flesh flew up and filled the air like dust. In reply to his question, Teng Lān Kat was told that those subjected to this torture had shown no care for parents, and were quite void of natural affection. If filial piety is the chief of virtues, the absence of it must be the most heinous in all sins of omission. To receive for years the untold kindness of parents, and then drop them out of one's reckoning, is ungrateful forgetfulness ; to disregard their wishes and be stubborn and rebellious in temper is contempt for those who are nearest. He who sets at naught an emperor is beheaded, and is there to be no corresponding penalty for those who despise their parents? The Emperor distributes honours to those officials who assist him in the government; but, unlike parents, he does not give of his very heart's blood. The dog you rear will learn to drop his head and wag his tail in your presence, and the ox will bow itself to the yoke and patiently drag the plough; but when parents have nurtured a child, and he turns out worthless, dilatory, without any sign of natural affection in his behaviour, and treats those who have given him life and watched over him as though they were mere wayfarers or enemies, of all the thankless creatures in the universe such as he must be accounted the very worst.

After walking a few paces further, Teng Lān Kat asked, "Why are these bundles of clothes heaped up by the side of the passage?"

And the man in azure robes replied: "These belong to Buddhist priests and nuns who have been guilty of adultery. Guilt is increased tenfold when those who have taken the vows of Buddhism disregard them, and follow carnal indulgences in the name of piety and self-purification."

In reply to the question, "Are there not some who are good even amongst Buddhist nuns and priests?" the guide answers, "The good amongst them are either received into heaven or reborn upon earth amidst the most prosperous conditions. Those who are not good become either roving, hungry ghosts, or are changed into brute beasts."

Passing now into a yet lower sphere of punishment

upon turning a sharp bend in the path they saw a number of women almost entirely divested of clothing. Their skirts and hairpins and tunics and shoes were put aside in a great heap, and they were clad in slight waistcloths only. The ox-faced demons clutched the women by the hair and dragged them to the mouth of a mill some eighteen inches in diameter, just about wide enough, in fact, to admit a human body. The victims cried pitifully, and with many tears shouted, "Save life!" and in their agony held on to the lower part of the mill and resisted the attempt to thrust them into the funnels by which the mills were fed. The demons then put forth their strength, lifted them up and thrust them in head first, with feet pointing to the skies, and rushed madly round to turn the mill. So dreadful was the sight that the eye could scarcely bear to look upon it. Women were also brought and placed in troughs or mortars four or five feet in breadth. These also fought against their doom, and, rolling upon the ground, screamed wildly for help. Two demons, one grasping the head and the other the feet, took them and flung them into the trough. Upon being put into the trough or mortar, the hammer fell with a thud, and at each stroke they uttered several cries, at the same time stretching out their hands wildly and kicking about with their feet, whilst blood and flesh flew up in clouds.

As he turned his face aside and walked away, Lān Kat asked, "Why are women subjected to these terrible pains? for by nature they are gentle and free from vice, and they rarely practise what is wicked or outrageous, and extort and oppress. What reason can there be for the punishment they suffer? There is something inexplicable in all this."

The man in azure raiment answered: "Whilst the virtues of good women are known and appreciated by all, the vices of bad women are for the most part hidden from us. Some set themselves against their husbands who have taken concubines to continue posterity, and hope that the sacrificial service expected from descendants may cease. Others are angry with husbands who contribute to the support of parents, and would treat with the utmost meanness the aged representatives of the husband's family. As the result of all this, friends and kindred become divided, and resentments exist where there should be only kindness. Such offences are beyond the reach both of imperial law and family discipline, but they must be dealt with in the underworld."

Fifth Realm of Punishment.

Teng Lān Kat was then conducted to the fifth circle of punishment, where he saw forty or fifty great furnaces alight with caldrons of hot, hissing and boiling oil. Stepping near, he observed countless human forms rising up with the bubbling liquid, groaning, weeping, floating to the surface sinking again, and bone and flesh just falling to pieces.

To the question, "Who are these offenders?" the man in azure replied, "These are chiefly the little tyrants and impostors of the villages."

He then asked, "How is it that they can utter these distressful cries and have some kind of consciousness of pain?"

And it was answered: "In the world of the living, inasmuch as the body is regarded as the nearest and most substantial thing, it is the practice to feed its blood and skin and flesh and animal forces, to the neglect of the pure and subtle energies of the soul. But it is through the soul that men have the understanding in virtue of which they can eat and drink and walk and run. It is by the soul that a man can enter heaven or penetrate the earth, and receive either pleasure or pain. When the soul has once taken its departure, the body can no longer eat or drink or walk or run. It has become useless, and whether the bones have been dissolved and the form has been dissipated is a matter of little account. Although the corpse may be quite intact, mouth cannot speak, nor ear hear, nor feet walk; no answer being returned when questions are asked, and no pain felt when blows are given. The reason why there was consciousness of pain in life was that the soul was present, and the reason that there is no sense of pain in the body when death has taken place is that the soul has fled. But now that the body can no longer move, the form of the soul can pass about at will; now that the body is no longer able to eat, the form of the soul can perceive the incense burned in worship; now that the body can no longer speak, the voices of souls may be heard on still nights; and the dead flesh no longer being conscious of pain, the soul is alive to it. It is the soul passed into Sheol, alive and awake, which is burned and boiled and scourged. We speak of decomposing flesh, but never of decomposing spirit; of deceased bodies, but never of deceased souls. That which cannot die must always live, and that which cannot corrupt must always continue; this is the basis of transmigration, as well as the explanation of these soul tortures in the furnaces, in all of which the consciousness of pain is present. In ancient times there were those who accepted death in the pursuit of duty, and the trunk was left in one place and the head in another. When faithful ministers and true-hearted husbands and chaste wives, who were cut to pieces by the sword rather than allow themselves to be dishonoured, were subsequently made the objects of worship, are their images ever represented as headless? Whence it may be known that the soul-form cannot be divided like the body. When the body has been cut asunder, it cannot be joined together again; but with the soul it is as when one cleaves a column of smoke with a sword, or passes a silk thread through water. Immediate reunion of that which was divided takes place. If it were not so, when these materialised souls are disembowelled or have their tongues plucked out in the realms of Sheol, and transmigration subsequently takes place, they would have no sense of taste, nor would they know when their stomachs had been filled."

At this point in the discourse Teng Lān Kat jumped and clapped his hands, and exclaimed, "Well debated! Good doctrine, indeed! No wonder that your vocation in life was that of a scholar. This half day's talk I have had with you has so refreshed my mind and opened my understanding that it is better than ten years of study. By your kind permission I will now return home."

The man in azure raiment said, "You have not seen half of the eighteen Purgatories. Why need you be so impatient to go back again? I will now take you to see the sixth realm."

Lān Kat had no desire to go, but the man in azure raiment took him by the hand and dragged him along quite importunately.

Sixth Realm of Punishment.

Upon entering the sixth realm, groups of men and women were seen in standing, sitting, or reclining postures, all of whom had nails driven into hands, head, feet, or bodies; and, lo! a sight that was more startling still. After a certain turn in the pathway had been passed, Teng Lān Kat suddenly beheld his own brother's wife sitting on a flat stone with her feet in fetters, and a long iron nail driven into her left breast. He was greatly affrighted, and perspiration stood on his brow as he exclaimed, "Alas! alas!

What strange thing is this? When I left home this morning, I remember that my sister-in-law was lying in bed crying out with pain. It cannot surely be that she has died in the interval." And tears at once fell and flooded his face.

The man in azure raiment said, "Is this really your sister-in-law?" And Lān Kat answered in the affirmative.

At this point the guard interposed and said, "Your sister-in-law is not dead. This is the spirit-form (the astral body) of one who is still living."

Lān Kat asked, "How long is it since she was dragged in here?"

"About three years," the sentinel replied.

"No wonder," observed Lān Kat, "that my sister-in-law has had for that period a cancer in her left breast which has defied cure. All kinds of remedies have been tried, but in vain; and good and evil spirits alike have been worshipped, but the issue has been only vexation and disappointment. Who could have imagined that a demon in Hades had transfixed her? The æons of retribution are indeed difficult to escape. But what, after all, has been the sin committed by my sister-in-law that she must needs be tormented after this fashion?"

The guard replied: "It is secret malignity of which your sister-in-law has been guilty. Your brother having no issue by his wife took a concubine, who in due time bore him a son. The wife, fearing lest the concubine should be elated by the fact that she had brought the coveted heir to the family, and, presuming upon her position, become arrogant, on the third morning after the birth of the child entered the concubine's room, and, looking about to see that no one was near, drew forth an embroidery needle and ran it into the child. The babe uttered a broken cry, and the mother upon her return thought the child must have received some accidental injury at birth. The infant would take no nourishment, and cried without ceasing. After a day and a night it died, and the concubine was inconsolable at the disappointment to her hopes. The God of the Kitchen reported this matter to Wong Tai, and an order was issued to the powers of the underworld to deal with the crime. As she had pierced the child with an embroidery needle, Yama directed that her breast should be pierced with a nail. Is not retribution a fact?"

"Indeed! indeed!" exclaimed Lān Kat. "Who could have dreamed that she would have been so malicious? Heaven is not the sightless nonentity many suppose. No wonder that she has been afflicted so terribly. For the dead there is no resurrection; but now my sister-in-law, having endured this three years' punishment, may surely be allowed some little alleviation. May I request you to tell me by what means this nail may be withdrawn from her flesh? Have you the power to do it?"

The sentinel replied, "I am unable to do any such

thing upon my own responsibility, but have always to wait for the judge's orders."

"Is there nothing else you can suggest?" asked Lān Kat.

To which the sentinel returned answer, "To secure the removal of the nail, exhort her to repent, and possibly in the end her offence may be forgiven."

"The counsel is reasonable," said Lān Kat. "But it must be getting near nightfall, and I cannot stay to see more. I must hurry away home at once."

The man in azure raiment said, "I will take you back."

Conversing together as they walked, they soon found themselves once more at the top of the mountain, when the ghostly guide said, "Adieu. We may have some further opportunity of meeting."

And Teng Lān Kat said, "I am greatly obliged to you, respected brother, for your kind escort."

Just then a bird began to pipe, and he suddenly awoke. The wine-jar was turned upside down on the ground, the wine was all gone, and the sun was half down the western hills. Lifting up his heels as nimbly as he could, Lān Kat made the best of his way home.

Just as he was entering the house, he heard his sister-in-law abusing the concubine because her medicine had not been properly prepared, and insinuating that the concubine was trying to kill her, so that she might step into her authority as head of the house. Lān Kat remonstrated, and said, "Do not be so angry, but try and cultivate a little quietness and self-restraint."

The sister-in-law replied, " I am in great pain, and when she provokes me by her blundering, how can I be expected to bear it ? "

" There was a time when you were not suffering," said Lān Kat. " Whatever pain you have to bear is of your own choice and seeking."

" Where indeed have I been to seek this trouble ? " said the afflicted woman. " Your brother treats me as though I were scarcely human, the concubine pays me no attention, and it is scarcely in the tone due to a sister-in-law that you address me. I see through it perfectly well. All the members of the family want me to die."

Lān Kat bluntly answered, " You are in just the same condition as though you *were* dead, notwithstanding the fact that you are still alive."

" And how is it, pray," she asked, " that I am in one and the same condition as though actually dead ? "

Lān Kat answered, " Your soul has been already snatched down into Hades and tortured there for three years past."

The exasperated woman then shouted out, " Have you seen my soul ? "

" Yes, I have," Lān Kat answered. " I recognised it there."

" In what way did you come to see it ? "

The story of the pilgrimage to the mountain, the

encounter with the man in azure raiment, and the visit to the underworld, with the sight that there met him of his transfixed sister-in-law, was then told in answer to the question.

"Of what offence had I been guilty, that they transfixed me?" asked the sister-in-law.

"Of a secret crime."

"I guilty of a secret crime? Have I been a cannibal, or biting any of you?"

"You took my little nephew and put him to death, and Heaven cannot pass by an act like that."

Striking the bed in her rage, she cried out: "Heaven and earth conspire to wrong me. Everybody knows your little nephew died an untimely death. When you say that I wrought him harm, you have surely lost your senses. Is my disposition of that sort, indeed? How many tears have I shed for the child—tears that are not yet dry? The very mention of his name stabs my breast with pain, and you say I was cruel. What proof have you? Speak out, and I shall be satisfied. If you defame me, you will die before me."

Lān Kat then laughed and said: "Sister-in-law, you are kind-hearted, indeed! When my brother's concubine bore a comely son, envy arose within you. Three mornings after his birth, you entered the room, took up the child, and, whilst crooning softly, you inflicted a fatal wound with your embroidery needle, and the poor thing never ceased crying till death brought release. Is that being cruel? or is it not?"

Hearing thus far, she was much afraid, her face grew quite livid, and she cried, "Do not libel me thus, or a thunderbolt may strike you."

Lān Kat answered: "There is no fear lest the god of thunder should aim his bolts at me, but Yama has already been compelled to transfix you. Were you guilty of this deed or not? Your own heart knows. I had no previous information about the matter, and have only been informed to-day. If my brother had had timely knowledge of your disposition, he would have dealt pretty roughly with you, I will be bound. Your pain, I fear, will be fatal, and all medicines prove useless."

As soon as the sin was brought home to the sister-in-law, her mouth relaxed, her voice dropped to a whisper, and she asked, "Is it then really true?"

"Of course it is. Do you imagine I am trying to frighten you?"

She then gasped: "It is not that you are trying to frighten me. As I heard you speak, I had my own fears that a judgment was resting upon me. If it is untrue, why should the crowds of doctors, exorcists, and necromancers we employed have failed to afford me the slightest amount of relief? If, however, you saw the nail you describe driven through my soul-form, why did you not try and draw it out for me?"

"I wished to draw it out, but the gaoler would not allow me."

"Am I doomed, then, to die in pain?" asked the sister-in-law. "For three years I have endured agonies that have wasted away my spirit. Is there no resource still left me?"

"If you change your disposition and guard against all malignity, possibly you may recover; but that is not at all certain."

With this he shook down his tunic sleeve, and went out of the door.

Turning restlessly in bed, and musing uneasily upon these matters, the sister-in-law admitted to herself that whatever had come upon her was through her own fault. "Kind-hearted women are delighted when the news is announced that their relatives have borne children, and send presents of pork or poultry for the festivities which celebrate the attainment of the first month of the infant's age. But I accounted my husband's concubine an enemy because she had borne a son, and that son moreover might have become rich and maintained me, and have married a wife who would have acted as my servant. And if he had been appointed a mandarin, I should have been first raised to rank, and for a century afterwards I should have been worshipped, and public business would have been suspended on the anniversary of my death. If I had not put him to death, he would now have been three or four years of age, and would have been able to come up to the bedside to ask after my health; and if I should die, there would have been a son to present offerings before my tablet, and, clothed in the white of mourning, and with bent back and dropped head, he would have cried, 'My mother! Alas! my mother!'"

As she thought thus, her tears began to run in unceasing streams, and, putting her hands before her mouth, she said in smothered tones, "Child, I know that you died in pain, and I regret the distress which I caused to your poor mother. As your spirit wanders beneath the Nine Fountains, do not cherish resentment against me." When she had thus spoken, she continued to shed tears in silence.

In a little time she dried her eyes, and sent a slave-girl to buy candles for worship; and when she had lighted them in the open court, she made the slave-girl help her to walk forth, and then she knelt, knocked her head on the ground, and offered up a secret petition for mercy. So earnest was she in her prostrations that she beat her brow on the ground till it was covered with dust and raised into large lumps and bruises.

After this religious act she was helped back to bed, where she passed through a great mental conflict, accompanied by groans and copious perspiration, the effect of which was to entirely change and humanise her disposition. Henceforth she treated the concubine as gently as though she were her own sister, and with a most perfect command of temper allayed any feuds that might threaten to appear in the household. She had no longer any desire to call in doctors to deal with her malady, for in confessing her own fault she was assured that she had found the true clue to her trouble. Against all human expectation, after ten days a skin formed over the open sore, as though unseen spirits were helping on the kindly process. Her progress in virtue and usefulness became more marked every day, and before three years had elapsed, wife and concubine each bore sons, who in due time became quite eminent in literature. Whilst yet living she had suffered the torments of Hades; but the narrative of her brother-in-law brought her to repentance, and then the gods were reconciled, and the light of spring stole back into her face.

"The editor of this series of Handbooks is to be heartily congratulated. He has chosen his subjects well, and he has chosen the right men for them."—*The Expository Times.*

BOOKS FOR BIBLE STUDENTS.
Editor: Rev. ARTHUR E. GREGORY.

THE SWEET SINGER OF ISRAEL. Selected Psalms, illustrative of David's Character and History, with Metrical Paraphrases. By BENJAMIN GREGORY, D.D. 2s. 6d.

"It contains some excellent specimens of the best kind of devotional commenting. Of parade of scholarship there is none; of its patience and accuracy, evidences are to be found on almost every page. The charm of the paraphrases increases as the reader recognises more clearly each time of reading their high quality as poetry, and their adequacy as an exhibition of David's actual thoughts. But it is in the devotional commenting that the excellence of the book especially lies. Illustrations from a wide range of literature and from an intimate acquaintance with human nature play about the passages, bringing out the truthfulness to life of their teaching, and its serviceableness to the soul. It is a choice book, fresh, rich, vigorous, 'honey out of the rock' served up with 'the fat of the wheat'; and its venerable author could hardly better crown his great services to the Churches than by giving them more."—Professor Moss in *The Preacher's Magazine.*

THE PRAISES OF ISRAEL: An Introduction to the Study of the Psalms. By W. T. DAVISON, M.A., D.D. *Third Thousand.* 2s. 6d.

Dr. MARCUS DODS writes: "As nearly perfect as a manual can be. It is the work of a reverent and open-minded scholar, who has spared no pains to compress into this small volume the best information and the most trustworthy results arrived at by himself and other experts."

"It gives all that is most required and most apposite in an Introduction to the Study of the Psalms. It gives this in admirable form; everywhere it furnishes the results of the best scholarship without the parade of learning."—*Critical Review.*

THE WISDOM LITERATURE OF THE OLD TESTAMENT. By W. T. DAVISON, M.A., D.D. *Second Thousand.* 2s. 6d.

"Dr. Davison has followed up his attractive volume in *The Praises of Israel* by another equally attractive. These are amongst the best contributions to the series."—*Critical Review.*

"It will take its place among those modern 'Helps' to the interpretation of Scripture which place the English reader almost on a level with those who can read the Bible in its original languages."—*Methodist Times.*

FROM MALACHI TO MATTHEW: Outlines of the History of Judea from 440 to 4 B.C. By Professor R. WADDY MOSS. *Second Thousand.* 2s. 6d.

"Mr. Moss's book is worthy of the series. His style is straightforward and graphic. He can tell a story rapidly and forcibly. There is vigour and there is vitality throughout. It is to be hoped that these manuals will be largely used."—*The British Weekly.*

*

BOOKS FOR BIBLE STUDENTS—*Continued.*

AN INTRODUCTION TO THE STUDY OF HEBREW.
By J. T. L. MAGGS, B.A., Prizeman in Hebrew and New Testament Greek, London University. Small crown 8vo, 5s.

Rev. W. F. MOULTON, D.D., says: "I do not know any book within the same compass which approaches this in usefulness for the beginner. The Reading Lessons, fully annotated and supplied with references to the sections of the grammar, will prove of great service. I heartily congratulate the editor of the series on securing the aid of so able and scholarly a writer."

Canon DRIVER says: "Would prove to be well adapted for the class of students whose needs it is designed to meet."

IN THE APOSTOLIC AGE: The Churches and the Doctrine.
By R. A. WATSON, M.A., D.D. 2s. 6d.

"Well fitted to be used as a text-book.... Every reader will be thankful for so vigorous, fresh, and candid a treatment of the most important period of the life of Church and doctrine."—*The Expositor.*

"Certainly one of the ablest books in the series. Dr. Watson is a powerful and courageous thinker, furnished with competent scholarship and knowledge. The book addresses itself to the Bible student, and directs his attention to matters that require to be noted at the outset of his studies in Church History. Its method is as instructive as its substance."—*Wesleyan Methodist Magazine.*

THE GOSPEL OF ST. JOHN: An Exposition, with Short Notes.
By THOS. F. LOCKYER, B.A. *Second Thousand.* 2s. 6d.

"A terse, fresh, and thoughtful exposition of the Gospel of John. Every preacher will find useful hints in it, and the price is amazingly low—over three hundred pages for half-a-crown. It deserves to have a wide circulation."—*The British Weekly.*

THE EPISTLES OF PAUL THE APOSTLE: A Sketch of their Origin and Contents.
By GEORGE G. FINDLAY, B.A. *Fourth Thousand.* 2s. 6d.

"The reader will find here compressed into a small space what he must otherwise seek through many volumes.... Mr. Findlay has before now proved himself an able and accomplished expositor of St. Paul, and this little work will fully maintain his character."—*The Scotsman.*

THE THEOLOGICAL STUDENT: A Handbook of Elementary Theology.
By J. ROBINSON GREGORY. *Fourth Thousand.* 2s. 6d.

An Explanatory Index of Theological Terms and a very full list of Questions for Self-Examination add greatly to the practical value of the book.

"Mr. Gregory is ... a born and trained theologian. Some departments he has made well-nigh his own—especially the doctrine of the Last Things. And better than that, he can write for beginners."—*The Expository Times.*

THE LAY PREACHER'S HANDBOOK; First Steps in Homiletics. By Rev. C. O. ELDRIDGE, B.A., with Preface by Rev. ARTHUR E. GREGORY. *Third Thousand.* Small crown 8vo, 2s.

"'Beauty for Ashes' would describe the change which would come to some pulpits, if only the men who preach would take to heart the instructions given in this book."—*Joyful News.*

"Written with care, ease, and simplicity, and is just the book we should like to see in the hands of all young men beginning to preach."—*Preacher's Magazine.*

"Admirably adapted to the needs of our own local preachers. . . . The book does not consist of pious platitudes; from beginning to end it is practical and sensible."—*Methodist Recorder.*

"Clear, sensible, practical."—*North British Daily Mail.*

THE STUDY OF THE BIBLE: An Address to Lay Preachers. By Rev. Professor G. G. FINDLAY, B.A. 48 pp. small crown 8vo. Paper covers, 6d.

Professor W. T. DAVIDSON, D.D., says: "Admirably suited as an elementary guide to the study of the Scriptures, for the class for whom it was written.

The Preacher's Magazine

UNION FOR BIBLICAL AND HOMILETIC STUDY.

1.—The OBJECT of the Union is to help its members in systematic Biblical and Homiletic studies.

2.—Correspondence Classes are formed, under the guidance of competent tutors, in the following subjects: 1. Homiletics. 2. Systematic Theology. 3. Bible Study. 4. New Testament Greek. 5. Elementary Hebrew. 6. Christian Evidences. 7. Church History.

3.—The Union is started in connection with *The Preacher's Magazine*, and a portion of that journal is reserved for papers written specially for the members. *The Preacher's Magazine* is the ordinary means of communication between leaders of classes and their members. Members of the Union are entitled to receive answers to questions, criticisms of outlines, etc.

4.—Membership is open to all Christian workers.

5.—In order to cover the necessary expenses of postage, etc., members of the Union are asked to subscribe *not less* than Sixpence per annum.

General Secretary: Rev. ARTHUR E. GREGORY.

COURSES OF STUDY.

1. **Homiletics:** Tutors—Revs. C. O. ELDRIDGE, B.A., D. BROOK, M.A. B.C.L., J. EDWARDS, W. A. LABRUM.
2. **Systematic Theology:** Tutor—Rev. J. R. GREGORY.
3. **Bible Study:** Examiner—Rev. Professor FINDLAY, B.A.
4. **New Testament Greek** (Advanced)—Rev. R. M. POPE, M.A. ; (Elementary)—Revs. A. H. WALKER, B.A., and A. W. COOKE, M.A.
    Fee for the Greek Courses, 5s. (including text-book).
5. **Elementary Hebrew:** Tutor—Rev. J. T. L. MAGGS, B.A.
    Fee for the Hebrew Course, 5s. (including text-book).
6. **Christian Evidences:** Tutor—Rev. S. E. KEEBLE.
7. **Church History:** Tutor—Rev. Professor J. G. TASKER.

For further information, see *The Preacher's Magazine.* (Price Fourpence.)

London: CHARLES H. KELLY, 2, Castle St., City Road, E.C.; and 66, Paternoster Row, E.C.

"*The Preacher's Magazine* maintains its place as the first of the homiletic monthlies, and the rest are not in sight."—*Expository Times*.

The Preacher's Magazine.

FOR PREACHERS, TEACHERS, AND BIBLE STUDENTS.

PRICE FOURPENCE MONTHLY.

Editors: MARK GUY PEARSE and ARTHUR E. GREGORY.

Amongst the Contributors are

The Very Rev. C. J. VAUGHAN, D.D.
Ven. ARCHDEACON FARRAR, D.D.
W. HAY M. H. AITKEN, M.A.
Professor J. AGAR BEET, D.D.
DAVID BROOK, M.A., B.C.L.
ARCHIBALD G. BROWN.
JOHN CLIFFORD, D.D.
WILLIAM CUFF.
W. H. DALLINGER, LL.D., F.R.S.
W. T. DAVISON, D.D.
W. J. DAWSON.
Professor G. G. FINDLAY, B.A.
CHARLES GARRETT.
Professor A. S. GEDEN, M.A.
J. MONRO GIBSON, D.D.
BENJAMIN GREGORY, D.D.
F. HARPER, M.A.
R. F. HORTON, D.D.
H. P. HUGHES, M.A.

CHARLES LEACH, D.D.
J. SCOTT LIDGETT, M.A.
J. T. L. MAGGS, B.A.
Professor R. WADDY MOSS.
J. HOPE MOULTON, M.A.
CHARLES NEW.
JOSEPH PARKER, D.D.
T. G. SELBY.
W. SPIERS, M.A., F.G.S.
Professor W. F. SLATER, M.A.
H. ARTHUR SMITH, M.A.
JAMES STALKER, D.D.
Professor G. T. STOKES, D.D.
T. BOWMAN STEPHENSON, LL.D.
Professor J. G. TASKER.
Principal T. VINCENT TYMMS.
R. A. WATSON, D.D.
W. L. WATKINSON.

OPINIONS OF THE PRESS, ETC.

Mr. Spurgeon: "As good as the *very best* of its homiletical compeers. It goes in for practical suggestion, which will be really useful to men labouring to save souls. We like such magazines, and feel helped by looking them through. Each number is a capital return for the money."

Professor J. A. Beet, D.D.: "This is a thoroughly good magazine. From end to end it is full of first-rate homiletic matter."

Dr. Charles Parkhurst (New York): "It is the best help of the kind I have seen for many a day."

Thomas Champness: "We especially recommend the younger men to buy this magazine. These are days when pulpit freshness is in demand, and we do well to read that which will suggest ideas we have not thought of, and which will strike our hearers by its freedom from mildew."

The Christian Leader: "A periodical of very high tone and wide sphere of usefulness. It has specially helpful notes and illustrations. . . . A brilliant monthly."

The Methodist Sunday School Record: "The very best thing we have seen in the way of suggestiveness for workers, preachers, and teachers for Children's Sunday is furnished in the *Preacher's Magazine*."

Sent Post Free for Twelve Months for 4s.
Specimen Copy post free for Fourpence.

LONDON: C. H. KELLY, 2, CASTLE STREET, CITY ROAD, E.C.;
AND 66, PATERNOSTER ROW, E.C.

www.ingramcontent.com/pod-product-compliance
Lightning Source LLC
Chambersburg PA
CBHW032224230426
43666CB00033B/1160